Luminos is the open access monograph publishing program from UC Press. Luminos provides a framework for preserving and reinvigorating monograph publishing for the future and increases the reach and visibility of important scholarly work. Titles published in the UC Press Luminos model are published with the same high standards for selection, peer review, production, and marketing as those in our traditional program. www.luminosoa.org

THE FLETCHER JONES FOUNDATION

HUMANITIES IMPRINT

The Fletcher Jones Foundation has endowed this imprint to foster
innovative and enduring scholarship in the humanities.

Almost Hollywood,
Nearly New Orleans

The publisher gratefully acknowledges the generous support of the
Fletcher Jones Foundation Humanities Endowment Fund of the
University of California Press Foundation.

Almost Hollywood, Nearly New Orleans

The Lure of the Local Film Economy

———

Vicki Mayer

UNIVERSITY OF CALIFORNIA PRESS

University of California Press, one of the most distinguished university presses in the United States, enriches lives around the world by advancing scholarship in the humanities, social sciences, and natural sciences. Its activities are supported by the UC Press Foundation and by philanthropic contributions from individuals and institutions. For more information, visit www.ucpress.edu.

University of California Press
Oakland, California

Suggested citation: Mayer, Vicki. *Almost Hollywood, nearly New Orleans: the lure of the local film economy*. Oakland: University of California Press, 2017. DOI: https://doi.org/10.1525/luminos.25

Library of Congress Cataloging-in-Publication Data

Names: Mayer, Vicki, 1971- author.
Title: Almost Hollywood, nearly New Orleans : the lure of the local film economy / Vicki Mayer.
Description: Oakland, California : University of California Press, [2017] | Includes bibliographical references and index.
Identifiers: LCCN 2016046883 (print) | LCCN 2016048419 (ebook) | ISBN 9780520293816 (pbk. : alk. paper) | ISBN 9780520967175 (ebook)
Subjects: LCSH: Motion picture industry—Louisiana—New Orleans.
Classification: LCC PN1993.5.U744 M39 2017 (print) | LCC PN1993.5.U744 (ebook) | DDC 791.4309763/35--dc23
LC record available at https://lccn.loc.gov/2016046883

26 25 24 23 22 21 20 19 18 17
10 9 8 7 6 5 4 3 2 1

CONTENTS

ACKNOWLEDGMENTS

I didn't set out to write another book. After Katrina and amidst my own trauma, I took refuge in the archives of the Louisiana Research Collection at Tulane University. There I immersed myself in the local film economy of the 1900s, but when I emerged I confronted the film economy of today. Whether through loving or loathing, labor or leisure, everyone I knew was talking about the experiences of living in Hollywood South. This unexpected collision of my scholarly and personal worlds produced the story I tell here about film, creative economies, and the city I moved to in 2003.

Along the way, I have had funding and research support through many of Tulane's institutions and colleges. In particular, I would like to thank the School of Liberal Arts (SLA), the New Orleans Center for the Study of the Gulf South, the Murphy Institute, and the Phyllis M. Taylor Center for Design Thinking, through which I received an endowment on behalf of the Louise and Leonard Riggio Professorship and the Carnegie Foundation. Together, SLA and the endowment via the Taylor Center allowed this project to be published as an open-access monograph.

I am forever grateful to the many people who have encouraged me along the way and contributed to this work. They have given me access to their knowledge about the numerous ways that the political economies of media impact and are impacted by the ways we feel about time, space, and place in cities. They have confided their own insights and emotions around the experiences of Hollywood South, from the episodic to the ephemeral. Although the argument in this project is my own, I hope I have rendered their inputs and voices faithfully.

Finally, this work is dedicated to all the creative people of New Orleans, including and especially Tor and Liina.

I'm Just a Film Tax Credit

(In homage to the television educational series *Schoolhouse Rock*)

Oh, I'm just a tax credit, only a tax credit, but certainly not sitting here alone. By 2012 my numbers had multiplied. Not only did I have a limitless number of siblings waiting to be chosen, but I was part of a family known as the Louisiana Entertainment Tax Credits and Incentives. Touring concerts and Broadway shows picked up the music and theatrical tax credits, while video-game and software studios brought back interactive-media tax credits. But I'm just a film tax credit, and I'm waiting here in Baton Rouge for my blockbuster to set me free. Chances are very good.

Two thousand miles away, there's a film-studio executive sitting in committee with a folder full of pitches, producers, and budget plans. They're all waiting too. Pitches and producers await the "greenlight" to start production, and the budget plans give the studio committee plenty of fodder for their decisions. Luckily, the executive already knows me and finds me quite attractive. After all, I was created to catch her eye. So I'm introduced to the committee, along with product sponsorship and synergies, licensing and distribution deals, and a host of other offsets and incentives for films. Each film project is so expensive. The price of star personnel, from the headliner talent to the brand-name director, has driven up costs—while global success banks on sunk costs, such as showy special effects and massive media promotion. The studio needs a film that acts like a tentpole to fund the future productions and products captured in its field of vision. Turns out, I'm the perfect match for a project set in Los Angeles when aliens attack. It's no big deal because I'm what the studio needs right now: to cut costs in production next year. Plus, our pairing brings all other sorts of gifts, as I assure the lenders and insurance companies of upfront money. A quick rewrite of the script and off I go.

First to the production balance sheet: there I'm on a fast track for state verification and approval. Along with the millions of fellow Louisiana tax credits, I may be California dreaming, but I stay in state, where I have the most value. You see, I may be leveraged for venture investment coming from Manhattan or Silicon Valley, but my value can only be claimed by a Louisiana citizen or corporation. The studio wants me, but not enough to move. Nor are they going to risk their future if my project is a flop. They are so fickle. So the studio leaves me in the hands of the producer, who forms a limited liability company (LLC) to meet me on location. The LLC is really agile, living fast and dying after the film is done and sold back to the studio. No matter. On location, I'm really useful, giving discounts on everything from the hired hands to the executive hotel suites where we stay. This is the most high-profile time in my life. The newspapers and trade press celebrate me as the star behind Hollywood South. It's a whirlwind, though, as the production company is rushing to shoot and post-produce as quickly as possible. I'm also nervous, because in order to go further, the project has to wrap. Luckily, we do it all in just a year. The state looks me over on the balance sheet again, where I've already been approved by the LLC's handpicked auditor. It's time to go underground.

The LLC leaves me with the tax-incentive broker. Even as good as I was to the producers, they still have not gotten their promised payout. Nor will they get it unless they sell me. Louisiana LLCs do not owe either state or federal taxes as corporations would. Even the producers will likely go home owing nothing to the state, as they are residents elsewhere. Instead they have to find a local buyer with personal or corporate tax liability. The matchmaking is overseen by a broker, who bundles me with other transferable tax incentives and sells me to the highest bidder. In the best-case scenario, my stated value is relatively unchanged. In the worst-case scenario, the state still guarantees that I'm worth at least 85 cents on the dollar. Turns out, however, there's no shortage of firms and their executives who would love even a 5 percent discount on their taxes for a year. The bigger the buyer's tax liability, the higher my value as the market tilts to the highest bidder. The broker also wants to see me off for as close as possible to my original promised value. That generally means the broker is seeking the richest person or most taxed company to take as many credits as possible without a hassle. My dance card is likely to be full of potential suitors from energy and chemical, oil and gas, and other infamous industries—but I actually don't know who will take me home. Though everyone seemed to know about me before I came to this eerie place, now it seems like no one really knows about me, except for a select handful of very powerful brokers, lawyers, and buyers whose names are not public information.

As I suspected, I'm sold, and even if no one else knows, I still sense my true worth. Someone in Hollywood sponsored a film, and someone in Louisiana paid a little less to the state till. While I reassure the financiers, on the front end, that they risk almost nothing, I can help industrial and corporate giants, on the back end, keep pace with those privileged investors who pay a lower tax rate than their employees. When I am finally cashed in, sometimes years later, I realize my new future with the "job creators." Who knows what well I might frack or whose office I might renovate? Sure, sounds more glamorous than sitting around in the state capitol waiting to get allocated to a health clinic or a community college. Though they may gripe about their budget shortfalls and reduced services, even local government leaders think I'm better off in someone else's pocket. After all, I have so many incentive friends in the film commissions and the municipal budget offices. Together, we have generated so many stories of local people. There's the one about the small-business guy who now monopolizes the trucking industry for film and television. And I love the ones about the baker who sold more cupcakes to a hungry film crew or the hotel concierge who does such a great job introducing our authentic cuisine. My favorite stories, though, are the ones about the Hollywood actors who lovingly restore one of our decaying mansions, not to mention the indebted students who dream of being as famous as the actors, right before they move to Southern California.

As for the film I helped make? We parted ways so long ago. I'm just a film tax credit.

Introduction

Presenting Hollywood South

Bells sounded in 2014 when a prominent service agency for film production in Los Angeles announced a report revealing that Louisiana had surpassed California as the top location for major film production. While the ringing in Southern California tolled the steady decline of the local film economy, it sounded more like wedding chimes in the Louisiana press. Headlines proclaimed that Louisiana had become the "Film Production Capital of the World."[1] Embedded in the euphoria over the state's film-production stature was a sense of achievement. Merely twelve years and over $1 billion in investments had paid off in the making of Hollywood South.

That Louisiana grew to become the third-largest economy for film production in the United States in less than a decade seems curious, if not counterintuitive, given the position of the state in economic terms and in the American popular imagination. In 2013 Louisiana continued to be one of the ten poorest states in the country; about one-fourth of the population resided in the New Orleans metropolitan area, where nearly 30 percent lived below the poverty line.[2] From 2010 to 2012, the state claimed that the film industry generated over $1.7 billion in revenues. Meanwhile, it slashed spending for higher education, health care, and social services to cover a little over $150 million in budget shortfalls.[3] A 2014 report by the state Legislative Auditor's Office found that budget cuts over the past eight years had rendered the Department of Children and Family Services unable to "fulfill their function." The halving of the state's higher-education budget from 2008 to 2015 led to the steepest rise in tuition and fee costs for public colleges in the United States, accompanied by exploding student loan debt, while keeping Louisiana at forty-eighth in graduation rates.[4] During the same period, the state increased funding for film and television production to more than $200 million.[5] These sad financial figures have been re-inforced in media images of a region crushed by Hurricane Katrina and successive hurricanes since 2005, the BP oil spill in 2010, and recurring political crises around graft and corruption.[6] In other words, visuals in the newspaper of red-carpet pre-mieres and star sightings, along with the endless stream of testimonials touting film-project budgets, sales receipts, and job numbers, sat alongside the uncomfort-able realities of "crisis ordinariness" that had come to characterize life for the aver-age Louisiana citizen.[7] How these two realities coexist, and even mutually reinforce each other, is the subject of this book.

From a purely rational standpoint, the growth of Hollywood film and televi-sion production in cash-poor states is the result of a supply-side economic strat-egy, what presidential candidate George H. W. Bush called "voodoo economics" in 1980. In 2012 alone, the film industry received $1.5 billion in state-based tax breaks.[8] The tradable film tax credit personified in the Prologue is but one ex-ample of welfare for the wealthy because it promises a break for corporations and their richest beneficiaries by minimizing their fiduciary responsibilities to states. Until the 2008 financial meltdown, the primary buyers of film tax credits in states with transferable programs were hedge fund investors, insurance companies, Wall Street banks, and private equity firms.[9] At a time of general budgetary austerity, states cannot fill the holes in their budgets by simply adding together the incomes and property taxes of film-industry employees. Instead, government officials justify the guaranteed future losses to the state coffers with another promise: a self-sustaining satellite of the Hollywood film economy. From there, any political debates around regional film policy get murkier, full of technocratic details of du-eling algorithms and doublespeak jargon. I've tried to decode some of the rhetoric typically used by the wonks for the dutiful citizen–reader in the Appendix, but a critical stance must tarry in the irrational as well.

The truth is that the little Hollywoods of the world—whether in the American South or South America—are based less on well-reasoned economic strategies for incentivizing an industry, and more on beautiful projections of what might be. Boosters point to the high costs and time involved in creating twentieth-century Hollywood as a regional growth engine, not only for film and television, but for a wide range of high-tech and creative industries that perpetuate a well-paid, highly skilled labor force in Southern California. The proximity of tourism and enter-tainment industries in that region further bolsters claims that film economies multiply profits by making desirable places to work, live, and visit. The vision of a carbon-neutral cluster of firms attracting venture capital and bringing back edu-cated workers makes both liberal and conservative politicos smile, especially after years of seeing their budgets unmade by shuttered factories, offshored industries, and a shrinking if not stagnant tax base. Working in tandem with the film studios' national trade organization, the Motion Picture Association of America (MPAA), regional film offices and state economic-development departments frequently stress the same financial indicators that the MPAA has used, first to lobby for Canadian tax breaks in the 1980s and then to respond to critics ever after: "Pure and simple: film and tax incentives create jobs, expand revenue pools, and stimulate local economies."[10] Even though every one of these assertions has been hotly debated in the corridors of state capitols and some academic enclaves, the public debate has been largely displaced by the dreams of a Hollywood-borne deus ex machina.

My modest goal in the chapters that follow is to have that discussion, based not on indicators, multipliers, future visions, or predictions, but on how life in a film economy shapes and is shaped by its location. As we know, location involves both history and geography, but it is also phenomenological, as in a sense of place. Hollywood South in this regard is never quite the same as Hollywood, even as it leverages the latter's power in transforming New Orleans. The city and the industry influence each other in ways we sense but can't always name. People frequently say their city is like a state of mind, but beyond the metaphorical, everyday life has temporal and spatial rhythms that are tethered not only to the conscious feelings we have about places, but also to the unconscious structures of governments and institutions, markets and economies. It is the thin line between feeling at home *(heimlich)* and feeling displaced—what Freud termed the "uncanny" *(unheimlich)*—because it reveals what we repress in wanting home.[11] *Almost Hollywood, Nearly New Orleans* delves into the ways in which the aura of Hollywood film production and the construction of a place called "New Orleans" conflict, disrupt, and disable each other—precisely because they repress their underlying power structures. Put plainly, it's the annoying little cultural disconnects in particular locations that get most folks riled about film policy and production economics.

In this respect, Louisiana and New Orleans are not unique in their status as places where we locate ourselves—even if New Orleanians may have their own unique contexts for seeing Hollywood at home. For myself, however, New Orleans makes sense as a case study of this dialectical relationship between film economy and location. The city predates Hollywood as a coveted spot for film producers, having piqued the interest of William Selig in 1907, right before he hightailed it to Los Angeles. The reason why he left is a key to both the success of the film economy in Southern California and its failure in Louisiana and elsewhere. For New Orleans continues to inspire cultural exceptionalism even as its policies mimic completely unexceptional schemes for segregating social classes, preserving white wealth and privilege, and profiting from black culture.[12] These factors also underline the rebirth of the regional film dreams that Louisiana would pioneer as an economic policy in the United States. By continually being first in offering among the most generous payouts around the globe, Louisiana catapulted the City of New Orleans into the spotlight as a low-cost leader for shooting Hollywood film and television. This happened soon after I had relocated to the city, and so I bore witness to the ways in which film production colluded with the worst horrors of the city's transformations in the past decade—even as it stood on its own stage as a protagonist for economic recovery. Before I tell the paradoxical tale of Hollywood South, though, let's return to Selig's story in the making of Hollywood.

HOLLYWOOD AS INDUSTRY AND AURA

The question of why Hollywood succeeded in Southern California, while other locations failed to gain traction as film capitals, has plagued historians across academic disciplines.[13] Despite the various hypotheses, however, one thing is certain. Once established, Hollywood became a self-perpetuating cluster of movie companies and film workers. Before that time, Selig found an arid brushscape lacking electricity, water, or any other infrastructure needed to grow any industry, creative or not.[14] The threat of fire and the unpredictability of earthquakes also lobbied against building an industry based on highly flammable celluloid. The hills of Edendale were about as far from financial resources and raw materials for filming as one could get in the continental United States. What the region did have was plenty of free land, cheap labor, and a municipal government and business community eager for a white, Protestant migration. Taxes were low, and wages were reportedly 25–50 percent lower in Los Angeles than in New York.[15] The Southern Railroad, in cahoots with the city, had just commissioned the Edison Company to shoot promotional reels targeting new migrants with sun, beaches, and virgin land for development.[16] It may be easy to forget that early independent producers in California favored the Western genre because they didn't need studio space to shoot it, but once studios dominated the landscape, shooting in house was more efficient. Time trumped space in the budget.[17] Selig's love of jungle movies did not send him packing to the tropics. He simply built a zoo on his studio grounds to house the monkeys and tigers.[18] Shooting on his own land, Selig had perfected the jungle film genre, recreating the subtropical place he had just fled, but for a fraction of the cost.

As settings could be increasingly fabricated, Southern California and the film industry became indivisible as a place of power called Hollywood. For most of the twentieth century, the metropolitan region was where film studios located and their employees resided, where distribution deals were made and projects took shape before production. In fact, nearly all of these financial operations and creative decisions still happen in Hollywood.[19] Film and media workers continue to flock to Los Angeles, drawn perhaps by the aura of film production. Once there, they find that their steady employment and their location are codependent. Whether in the skilled trades or in the creative arts, film workers find they must be close to the production hub to build both their credit sheets and the cultural bonds that communicate their dedication to new projects and their fellow crew members.[20] Yet, by the 1990s, the number of production hubs for Hollywood had multiplied across both state and national borders. It turns out that the economic values of the land and labor that drove the film industry to Southern California in the first place were as artificial as Selig's jungle movie sets.

Supported by Wall Street and protected by the Feds, Hollywood's concentration of resources was fueled by government policies that shielded competition abroad and allowed national oligopolies to form. During his first decade in California, Selig's business relied on the Motion Picture Patents Company (MPPC), which excluded foreign film companies and monopolized raw film stock and technologies. Known as the Edison Trust, MPPC was replaced by an even more potent, verticalized studio system that sought to dominate film production, distribution, and exhibition. The industry's trade association, the Motion Picture Producers and Distributors of America (MPPDA), worked hand in hand with the state to stave off censors and competition with their own Production Code. Even after the U.S. Department of Justice began targeting the trust-like activities of the largest studios, Congress still ensured that a cartel controlled foreign distribution and U.S. exports.[21] The MPPDA meanwhile grew a managerial class of investors based in Wall Street finance, while keeping the creative workforce in place, both literally and figuratively. The real "genius of the system," in the words of film historian Thomas Schatz, was the studios' use of assembly-line production to create film art.[22] Super profits from movie theaters were guaranteed by the block booking and the blind buying of cheap stock stories, enabling bigger budgets for expenditures elsewhere, generally on the copyrights for first-run films and the A-list stars that raised Hollywood's prestige. Selig also imagined that the production lots themselves could be a third line of income, for example by bringing in visitors to see the zoo as an attraction. Selig's dream never was realized personally. When his company was consumed by another one, he made a living selling the rights to stories he had bought cheaply from others and hoarded over the years.[23] His legacy lives on, instead, through a politics that benefits the industry, as much with regard to its famous moniker as to its infamous profits.

RETURN OF THE ZOMBIES

Associated with glamour and status, creativity and entrepreneurship, Hollywood now personified a protagonist in its own story, even as its doppelgangers in New York provided the crucial financial foundation. Throughout the golden age of cinema, the studios recreated low-budget jungles, castles, and other faraway lands, while a fantastic force of mummies, vampires, and zombies departed hallowed Hollywood in a scheme to dominate all media entertainment. The guaranteed double booking of these cheap filler films with their stock settings and characters offset any financial risks for their creators.[24] Having dominated the land, Hollywood mastered the labor power of the workers who made film art into an industry. Not so unlike the name-sake in the golden-age B movie of the same name, Hollywood had become the *King of the Zombies* (1941), with its crew of faithful laborers contained and protected on the same island. Then the zombies got loose.

The U.S. Supreme Court's 1948 decision to break up the vertical integration of the industry, combined with the growth of state-regulated national cinemas abroad and an upstart new broadcast medium, pushed Hollywood film production to new locales. Popularly called the *Paramount* decision, the ruling meant Hollywood's investors could no longer bank on guaranteed screenings at home or abroad, and instead they made distribution king across all entertainment media. The studios opted increasingly for fewer and flashier titles—and, later, branded properties that could tie together sales of film, television, music, games, and other amusements.[25] Meanwhile, the rebuilding of national cinemas in postwar locations, regulated public-service broadcasting, and new state financing models at least challenged Hollywood's colonization of all global screens. Seeing that the economic risks were greatest in making content, film studios thus withheld their largesse with production expenditures. In turn, producers struck out in search of ways to winnow their costs.

In setting the stage for the new regime in film economics, *King of the Zombies* was itself a pioneer of independent budget busting. Made by an outfit so under-funded that its kin were said to live in Hollywood's Poverty Row, *King* undercut even the cheapest of studio-made filler films for its theaters' double bills. The production house Monogram lacked the credit line of bigger studios. It was excluded from the majors' distribution networks and thus relied on unaffiliated movie theaters, generally in small towns or among second-rate chains.[26] So producers assumed all the risks of production up front. Avoiding payment for original content rights and drawing on a familiar roster of freelance workers, *King* was shot and finished in two weeks for a fraction of the cost of an average studio film.[27] By adding new themes and changing the setting, the film became the first of a series of zombie genre movies.[28] Monogram survived, just barely, by eating away at the margins of the studio film economy and by seizing on the antitrust pressures that slowly allowed Monogram to compete for second billings. The company reportedly made 10 percent of American films in the mid-1940s but only netted about $2,000 in profits per film.[29] Yet the company modeled how to be a low-price leader in production when the studios stood in the way of all other capital circuits.

The term *runaway production* sums up the results of the economic reorganization over the second half of the twentieth century. Cast outward from Hollywood with only a project contract in hand, film producers fled to places where they could find tangible benefits: stages and studios, professional trade workers, crew lodging and locational services.[30] Outside the United States, producers could build out the budget with foreign coproduction funds. Inside the country, hundreds of film commissions stood at the ready to offer producers free goods and services for projects that would shine a positive light on their regions. Riffing on the outsourcing waves in other industries, cultural scholar Toby Miller blames Hollywood for a New International Division of Cultural Labor, one in which producers leveraged places against each other in an effort to keep labor costs down and union power under control.[31] Balancing scheduling efficiencies and the clustering of film professionals with the lowest-cost locations and labor, independent producers by the late-1990s were flocking to a new model for financing location shooting, one that yoked the prospects of the producers to those of regions that hosted Hollywood projects.

Perhaps it was prescient that *Revenge of the Zombies* (1943), the sequel to *King,* was set in Louisiana. Looking and sounding almost exactly like its predecessor, *Revenge* adds a typecast collection of a mammy, a buffoon, and a creole spitfire along with sprinkled references to voodoo, the swamps, and the metropolis of New Orleans. Together, these locate the film's setting in a place.

HOME OF THE ZOMBIES

Of course, the idea that there is a force so dark that it feeds off the bodies of the powerless in a quest for immortality has been a motif in contemporary popular culture and fiscal policy. Both owe a debt to Hollywood and its modus operandi, which, in turn, owes a debt to a city that inspired an imaginative essayist by way of Cincinnati. Lafcadio Hearn, fan of occult and fable alike, came to New Orleans in 1876 seeking good stories and national audiences. He found both through his creative depictions of voodoo, a hybrid of various black religious rituals with colorful tropes born straight from the writer's desire for a place that was unlike all others. His tales of funerals, ghosts, and the undead conjured a potent image of an American city that was completely distinct—neither North nor South, neither East nor West—inventing "the notion of Louisiana, more specifically New Orleans, as idea and symbol."[32] It would seem logical that the first travelers seeking out authentic voodoo rituals soon followed.[33]

Along with George Washington Cable, Hearn, and other professional romantics of the place, the late-nineteenth-century chroniclers of New Orleans created the basis for a cultural economy built on the labors of authors and artists, playwrights and performers, as well as the industrial organization of publishers, printers, and publicists. That the first Vitagraph film-exhibition hall in the United States would be located in 1896 at the foot of Canal Street, which was an artery of the city's commercial heart, should be no surprise given the already thriving pulse of the theatrical sector there.[34] Sponsored by an elite class of philanthropic patrons, and with the backing of the largest newspaper chains, New Orleans's arts scene produced visions of an authentically distinct city that sold pottery and papers worldwide.[35] New Orleans's cultural economy succeeded in branding the city as a place where residual culture propelled its financial future. The geography of the city transformed to accommodate a residential boom driven by a white, middle-class exodus to new neighborhoods and new waves of white ethnic migrants who rented near the Central Business District and the French Quarter, the respective centers for commerce and culture.[36] By the 1940s, even the political and business leaders who shunned the mythologized creole culture concocted by writers and artists now wagered on "a nineteenth century urban fabric that could propel a tourism-based economy."[37]

At that juncture, *Revenge of the Zombies* appropriately brought together the mutable folk creature for tourists with an irrational love for the film industry. According to newspaper advertising, it played in New Orleans's movie theaters for eight months after its release, sometimes with top billing. Local critics seemed aware that the headlining star, John Carradine, had a theatrical career in New Orleans long before. More than that, the typecast characters and stereotypical tropes in *Revenge* seemed not so remote from those purveyed in the iconography of the tourism industry. Both Hollywood and the city itself trafficked in racialized images of "voodoo, jazz, Creole culture, decadence, sexual permissiveness, and exoticism" that mystified blackness for mass audiences while ignoring the contemporary realities of African-Americans.[38] They promoted a mental image of the place while concentrating profits among geographically distant elites. *Revenge* was one of some sixty films set in Louisiana during the height of the golden age of Hollywood.[39] For most of the movies, *Revenge* included, the production crews never stepped foot in the state, until state officials and Hollywood joined forces.

LEGISLATING HOLLYWOOD SOUTH

Although Louisiana had followed other states in using financial incentives for select place-based film projects, the 2002 Louisiana Motion Picture Incentive Act was the first statewide law in the nation crafted to satiate the needs of Hollywood's itinerant producers. It offered them guaranteed tax rebates for entire projects, based solely on production location and labor. The policy cribbed the language used by British Columbia, a Canadian hub for big-budget Hollywood film and television production, and set off a competition for domestic runaway production. Apart from this, what made the Louisiana law unique was its aspiration to grow a new permanent industry, one that would sustain a job cluster and spark an economic renaissance.

The path from Southern California back to Louisiana was paved by Lonny Kaufman. A former Hollywood executive, Kaufman came to head the newly formed arts-and-entertainment wing of the state's Department of Economic Development. In 2001, the state's economic development strategy still placed film alongside—of all things—coastal restoration as part of its vision: "To preserve, develop, promote, and celebrate Louisiana's natural and cultural assets for their recreation and aesthetic values."[40] That same year, the state appointed the Los Angeles–based Kaufman, who was then vice president of the second-largest payroll company for U.S. film workers and an ardent defender of the film industry. Joined by the obvious mutual interest in bringing Hollywood payrolls back within the national territory, Kaufman was charged with creating an arts-and-entertainment economic cluster that would drive development for years to come.[41]

His model for this endeavor was a new type of regional film economy that had transformed metropolitan Vancouver into "Hollywood North." Propped up by a low Canadian dollar and a fully refundable tax credit for a percentage of production services, Canada had opened the gateway for Hollywood producers to cut their costs in the late 1990s. By adding a local-labor tax credit, publicly subsidized infrastructure, and cheap transport routes, British Columbia had quickly surpassed other Canadian provinces that historically had more production facilities and crews. The credits, which were fully refundable at the end of the shoot, were the equivalent of outright grants to producers, who could then bank on them in finding loans. Vancouver experienced an economic boom as film projects lured both public and private investors in building a new home for the industry.[42]

In the wake of widespread layoffs and factory closures, Louisiana officials saw the potential for a film economy as a rising ship. Like many other states, Louisiana faced the challenge of paying for more with a stagnant, if not shrinking, tax base. The writ-large deregulation of federal social-welfare programs, beginning in the 1980s, pushed more economic responsibilities onto states and private citizens, incurring the greatest costs for those regions that had the least capacity to pay during tough economic downturns. Add to this the large-scale shuttering and offshoring of industrial firms, and suddenly, Los Angeles–based companies looked like attractive replacements.[43] The period following 9/11 was the high-water mark of a recession in Louisiana, which depended heavily on high oil prices and petrochemical industries.[44] Eyeing a new Hollywood hub, the state's then film commissioner, Mark Smith, glowed: "This industry has everything we want. Good pay. Advanced technology. It's a clean industry. It could stop the outmigration of talent from the state."[45] Over the objections of those involved in the state's indigenous music industry, these now commonplace arguments to seed a local film economy prevailed. Months later, a congressional special session put Kaufman's plans into motion in Louisiana.

The first iteration of Lousiana's transferable film tax-credit program beat the Canadians and set the standards for the ante in an incentives race. Unlike previous tax incentives, which targeted specific productions with place-friendly plotlines or cheap labor, Louisiana subsidized the *entire* production budget, from the first location-scout survey to the catered wrap party. The phrase "local labor" had a special cachet, not only for the extra earnings it awarded film producers, but also for the way it curried favor with national film-worker unions that were protesting foreign scabs. Plus, the credits were transferable, meaning the free money could be spread around the state to those who had nothing to do with the film industry (for examples, see the Prologue). With the support of the creative arts and fronting tax rebates for the rich, Louisiana liberals and conservatives lined up to support the measure.

On the surface, the careful alignment of external conditions with good governance seemed to produce a win–win for Hollywood and these other localities. Soon, states and municipalities across the country, many with little or no history of film production, followed suit. Before the 2009 economic crisis, forty-seven U.S. states offered substantial film-industry subsidies, either as a direct refund or as part of a brokered market.[46] The way each package worked was unique to the state, reflecting the political deals that each region negotiated to sustain the overall policy. Producers could use other states' programs as leverage for what they wanted to pay; for producers who would film in a particular location anyway, the money was pure windfall.[47] Statewide programs have been further enhanced by county and municipal tax programs aimed to lure locational shooting away from the obvious metro areas. Today, more than thirty-five states still compete in a race to the bottom for a film economy. The top contenders have been among the poorest U.S. territories: Georgia, New Mexico, Mississippi, Puerto Rico, and, of course, Louisiana. From 2008 to 2011, Michigan, with its notorious budget shortfalls, had the most generous tax-break program in the United States, using the state pension fund to pay back debt on a film-studio bond until the whole program was canceled out of financial exigency.[48]

The bidding war has meant that Louisiana had to dig deeper into the till to compete. In any given year, film tax incentives mean an overall loss of state revenues.[49] In the first eight years, Louisiana's "temporary" incentive expanded until it eventually became a permanent feature of the tax code. Legislators then succumbed to pressures from the music industry to extend credits to sound production and live performances. The film program is now one spoke in a wheel of entertainment tax credits that covers everything from video games and Broadway musicals to phone apps and human resources videos. On the local level, smaller cities and rural towns have posted giveaways for producers willing to ignore either New Orleans's dominant size and resources or Shreveport's proximity to Texas, where film crews have been based largely in the Austin–Houston–Dallas triangle. The size and scope of Hollywood giveaways made them vulnerable during the 2008 financial crash, when the national press raised concern about all state payouts for film production. The *New York Times* called the more than $27 million Louisiana refunded to the film *The Curious Case of Benjamin Button* "one of the most shocking bills" in light of the Wall Street bailouts.[50] The state responded by rescinding the sunset date for the policy.

New Orleans, meanwhile, looked further inward. Spurred by a federal initiative to better privatize the arts, and issued by the state's Lieutenant Governor's Office, the zombie economic plan, appropriately titled "Where Culture Means Business," directed the city to direct its biggest cultural tourism assets toward a future film economy. The report states: "Louisiana's tradition of spoken word lives on in traditional storytelling and contemporary coffee house poetry gatherings. The history of literary publications includes the 18th century Les Cenelles, published by Louisiana's free people of color. Louisiana continues to produce and attract writers whose work is celebrated at festivals named after William Faulkner, Tennessee Williams, or just, The Book. *Literature, in turn, underwrites a film industry* that has produced nearly 500 films in Louisiana."[51] Released one month before Katrina, the strategy became the city's wholesale when the waters receded and the lieutenant governor became New Orleans's mayor.

According to Chris Stelly, the current executive director of the state's Office of Entertainment Industry Development, 2011 marked the bellwether for the film economy, surpassing $1 billion in film project investment. Stelly touted that the industry is finally "stabilizing" in the region and showing "signs of being a consistent mainstay in the economy."[52] Along the way, the aspirations of the policy have been modified significantly. Statewide strategic plans no longer sought a permanent economic cluster by 2009. Shifting "pro" arguments from stable jobs to ephemeral status, the champion of public–private partnerships Louisiana Economic Development Corporation (LEDC) lumped film production together with industries that would spur the "creative class," a neologism that articulates the tastes and lifestyle habits of the urban, hip, youthful, and relatively affluent.[53] In the pretty but unsubstantive words of the LEDC, "A community with a strong creative class is a community with a future."[54] One of the devilish details, of course, is when the future will arrive. Supporters of the Louisiana program say that their "historic" advantage—two decades in 2018—will eventually prevail. And if we ever do get to that promised place, we should ask: What would be the costs?

That is the raison d'être of this book.

CLOSE-UP ON NEW ORLEANS'S FILM ECONOMY

In summary, the paradoxical story of Hollywood South is based on three realities that transcend Louisiana at the current moment. First, despite the claims around preserving what is distinctive about locations, the cultural economies rewrite local histories and their geographies to suit industrial aims. Second, cultural industries use the aura of their operations and products as leverage to reduce their economic costs in those same locations. Third, many people feel ambivalent about the first

FIGURE 1. A grocery clerk sports a photoplay-camera hairstyle to promote his aspirations to be a director in Hollywood South. Photo by Vicki Mayer.

two conditions for exploitation, based on the ways they see themselves and those around them participate in a local cultural economy, consenting to its systems of power in order to make do in increasingly crisis-ordinary times. Together, these realities have made Hollywood South another example of how "creative economy" strategies further allowed the extreme concentration of wealth under the twin banners of economic and cultural renewal—a point now admitted by the consultants to such claims.[55]

Yet, even if Louisiana's creative economy strategies are common in any global analysis, their unsurprising outcomes have been clouded by the stories of an exceptional New Orleans. The tensions between cultural policy, cultural industries, and the local culture where they are located bring us back to the first time New Orleans flirted with building a film economy. In the city, politicians have largely regarded the film industry as a salve, not a parasite. After Hurricane Katrina, the national press pithily predicted that the storm had "washed away" film production in the state. Following the first responders, Hollywood executives were among the first line of defenders of the city, calling for more investment, resources, and "commitment" to recovery.[56] Within a year, the number of film projects in the city surpassed those in the year before the storm. State leaders trumpeted the figure as a sign of an industry that was indefatigable in the city. Stelly boasted, "What couldn't kill it made it stronger in a way."[57] Like the zombies on the screen, the schemes to capture land and labor in the name of Hollywood seem ageless, even as their forms mutate.

What follows are three chapters that meditate on the strong pull of a film economy and its ability to transform the urban landscape while also mediating a sense of place. In other words, what is most compelling to me about the political economy of media production is its cultural impacts. From the halcyon boosterism that frames Hollywood projects in other locations, to the queasy uncanniness that subsequently infiltrates our sense of place, understanding film economies as cultural phenomena is no doubt both socially informed by my own status and subjectively interpreted through my own particular neuroses. Yet it seems to me that the absence of public debate around film tax incentives, especially in the wake of Occupy-like outcries, is precisely due to the lack of these more visceral linkages between public financing and the transformed feel of one's hometown or adopted location.

Chapter 1 examines the deep cultural origins of Hollywood South by looking back at the period when the fantasies associated with film economies first took hold. Recalling the filmmaker Selig and a host of those who followed him to New Orleans from 1900 to 1920 is a textbook lesson in how the film industry seeks market exclusivity, cheap production and labor costs, and a favorable political climate with plenty of public concessions. While political and economic conditions seemed promising to the producers and their boosters, it was ultimately not to be, for a number of reasons that give insight into the classic conundrum as to why Hollywood took root in Southern California and not anywhere else. In the case of New Orleans, the local politics of race, labor, and class staved off the efforts of the early film colonizers. The circulating visions of creolized paradise or peril constrained creative workers; or, in the words of one early-twentieth-century critic, the "local-color damnation of New Orleans was so complete it was virtually impossible for the imagination to transcend it."[58] In their push onward to Los Angeles, the filmmakers left the local ruling elites in charge of an economic strategy based mostly around land deals, wildcat speculation, and pyramid schemes. This historical cast, along with their tales of heroic entrepreneurialism and local boosterism, as well as greed and graft, might be considered allegories for Hollywood South today.

Since those early days, the switch from limited place-based film incentives to a universal schema for all major Hollywood production did not eliminate the industry's colonial ambitions over territory. Rather, it reoriented local space to more flexibly suit the needs of the professional managerial class more broadly. What emerges is a cultural geography for Hollywood South, which is the subject of chapter 2. Many of the requisite demands for a film economy are embedded in public–private partnerships, making them largely invisible to citizens, at least in the short term.[59] Hollywood studios' film production has reorganized the landscape of New Orleans through constant and yet ephemeral uses of public space. What citizens cannot witness, however, they can sense, in their movements around the city and their everyday routines. These sometimes strange or fleeting feelings, I would argue, highlight a critical ambivalence about film economies, one that needs to be elucidated as a first step toward political awareness. This chapter tracks these seemingly random patterns to show the ways in which Hollywood concentrates its capital in geographic clusters in the city through location shooting and housing. My data, including maps and photographs of film signs, demonstrate visually the unintended consequences of the film economy's success in terms of local neighborhoods and cultures. From this evidence, I argue that Hollywood South contributes to the governmental practice of privatizing public space.

This brings me to a deeper introspection about what the film economy means to ordinary citizens who live in its scope. Although my research has led me to believe that the current structuring of film incentives does more harm than good in New Orleans, I also understand the ambivalence that many feel, particularly those of us who see ourselves as creative or cultural workers in the city. Cultural economies are always double edged for cultural producers. We are drawn to preserve culture and place, even as our experiences and relationships there collude in their transformation. Film production operates according to the same logic. The ways in which film production appropriates local culture create an uncanny place that is both highly desirable and alienating. Chapter 3 relates the results of a three-year study of the local viewers of a television series that was produced in New Orleans and, to a large extent, for New Orleanians. *Treme* was an HBO production that addressed local cultural production and local creative producers. Set in post-Katrina New Orleans and shot concurrently with the rise of the film economy, the show drew many in the audience to do free or underpaid labor on the production's behalf. This chapter relates the diverse reactions of New Orleanians to the series, which is still held up as the best of what Hollywood South has to offer. By exploring notions of being and longing embedded in our sense of New Orleans as a place, this chapter exemplifies how we embrace, negotiate, and struggle with the aura of Hollywood South in our own ways.

Given this embeddedness, it is unclear how Louisiana can wean itself from dreams of a stable film economy. *Revenge of the Zombies* is perhaps not an authoritative source on this matter, but it does give a hint about how to stand up for ourselves. The obedient zombie wife turns on her master, leading to a denouement in which two of the African-American extras are leaving Louisiana and its crazy zombie culture behind. The chauffeur packs the car and tells the beautiful housemaid, "When I get you to Harlem I'm gonna get you a good job, a swell job. And if you save your money, aha, you and me we're gonna get married." To which she quips, "If I get the swell job, honey, I don't need to get married." The message for me is clear: if you can't beat the zombie master, you can at least find a better way out. For many people, the sticking proposition is the idea that film policy is a jobs policy. Like the housemaid, though, if we had good jobs independently, we wouldn't need a master.

This story of Hollywood South wraps with a more recent glimpse into the nature of regional film-policy politics, by discussing the state budget negotiations in the spring and summer of 2015. While there's been almost no public discussion of the zombie incentives, in Louisiana or anywhere else, pro-policy lobbyists hoped to curry favor by creating a high-pitched furor around jobs and creative opportunities. Their efforts demonstrate how hard it is to engage people seriously around media policy in the United States, especially when our feelings about who we are and how we want to live are pitted against the opaque and obscure language of a policy from which hope springs eternal. In response to this deep ambivalence, I ask whether it's not better to imagine alternative futures and creative economies with the potential to achieve the goals we seek for all citizens.

1

The Making of Regional Film Economies

Why La. Is Not L.A.

Whether we imagine new local film economies as runaways, satellites, or growing nodes in a global network, their creation and growth trace back to a genesis story of Hollywood. In this oft-told tale, a group of plucky entrepreneurs made their way from New York or Chicago to the promised land for film. Wooed by sunny weather, a diversity of filmic locations, and plenty of open land, they set up small shops that would, within a decade, become the grand studio system. Once clustered in the region, the efficiencies of sharing labor, land, and infrastructure made Hollywood *the* industrial production hub, to the exclusion of all others. It is a very compelling history, one that draws on narratives of individual innovation, environmental determinism, and the invisible hand of the market. It has been the dominant history that today guides cities vying for a film economy that, once planted, will germinate and grow into a self-sustaining industry.

This history is both true and false. While the beginnings of a film economy are no doubt rooted in these elements—the efforts of entrepreneurs, the conditions in a geographic region, and the economic principles of mass production—they are not in themselves sufficient. This history does not take into account the roles of government officials or other economic and cultural elites in cities. Most importantly, it cannot explain the ways that these social interactions drive speculation by reducing or increasing risks for film investors. In effect, the focus on the special case of Hollywood as the model story of a film economy directs our attention away from other histories, ones in which the film economy started, floundered, and failed, not once but repeatedly, over its own time scale. It is with these aims in mind that I turn to an alternative timeline of a film economy, one that begins and ends in the early twentieth century, only to be revived a century later in current film policies.

If we apply the basic principles that guided early moviemakers to what would become Hollywood, we could easily imagine that New Orleans would become a movie capital at some point around 1910. New Orleans had bright sunshine and mild winters, an enviable diversity of locations, and a massive real-estate inventory attributed to the drainage of the swampy surrounds. Indeed, most of the major producers of the time came through the city, announcing their plans to make their new home base there. By the end of 1915, these men had made their way to Los Angeles, leaving in their wake a local film industry that survived in fits and starts until 1920. The reasons why the former pioneers left, and why the latter locals failed, tell us about the ways in which political economy and culture are mutually imbricated. The perceptions of risks and benefits in speculative behavior are human, just as culture mediates the political and economic conditions for its own reproduction. This sense of the way a film economy is made of cultural perceptions that drive otherwise rational rent seeking should be part of a dialogue about film economies today.

NEW ORLEANS HISTORY AS MISE-EN-SCÈNE

This history takes place between 1909 and 1919 in two distinct and interrelated settings. Canal Street, the first setting, was located at the boundary between the historic but decrepit French Quarter and a new, modern business district. It was the economic heart of New Orleans, the Crescent City. Teeming with immigrants and sailors, native-born creoles, Anglos, and African-Americans, the street brought together people from around the world, even as its shops, hotels, and services would be segregated by race and social class. On the street, "Jewish, Italian, Chinese, and Negro working class children played, and their mothers conversed."[1] During Carnival season, Canal Street was the ceremonial promenade of the public spectacle. On hot summer days, patrons of all backgrounds went to catch a fifteen-minute film at one of the many movie theaters that lined the boulevard, including the very first Vitagraph theater in 1896.[2] Capital flowed to this area of the city in anticipation of an economic boom that would return New Orleans to its antebellum status as a world port. The eradication of yellow fever and public health campaigns were particularly important. Disease risked the decimation of the city's labor force and consumer base without notice. A predicted real estate boom led by theater investors evaporated after the rumors of the 1905 epidemic reached the North.[3] It would be the last outbreak. Further, the recent completion of the Public Belt railway, based on an efficient and centrally controlled ship-to-rail transport system, promised to attract new workers and visitors. Public officials and commercial elites prepared for the future population with plans to drain and develop some 25,000 acres that separated Canal Street downtown from the lake.[4]

FIGURE 2. Area targeted for neighborhood development in Bayou St. John in 1917. In Diamond Film Company, *Filmland: The Kingdom of Fabulous Fortunes* (New Orleans: Schumert-Warfield-Watson, 1917). Public domain. From Louisiana Research Collection, Special Collections Division, Tulane University Libraries.

Among this land was Bayou St. John, our second setting. This area was a narrow lake outlet connected to the Mississippi River via a sliver of raised land in an otherwise swampy area. Providing natural protection for boats, the bayou had been important to the early development of New Orleans. Now, however, the area was both underutilized and filthy. On the riverside bank, light industry connected to a freight railroad line and cargo holds on the water. Dumping and drainage polluted the waterway so badly that it would have to be closed for an environmental cleanup less than a decade later. Beyond this, development was sparse. Next to a marble yard sat a church, its orphanage, and horse stables. On the lakeside bank there were a few old plantation homes that owned the surrounding land, a rowing club, and a rifle range.[5] The area was known to many gentlemen a generation earlier as a secluded place to conduct duels. At this juncture, though, it was among the beacons for a widespread metamorphosis of the urban landscape. Land values soared as realtors predicted a housing boom that would extend from the busy downtown to the lakefront.[6] Farms parceled their land to eager developers. Planners had outlined a grid of streets extending up to City Park, a preeminent example of urban green space both in New Orleans and nationally. The redesign of the park's entrance and the addition of a neoclassical, marble peristyle and a Mission Revival–style casino exuded the elegance of urban leisure options for white elites. Lumber companies in the region mobilized for the incipient demand, which extended to a number of other, similarly positioned tracts around the city. The construction of the City Park neighborhood as an exclusive suburban enclave was complete by 1920.

Mayor Martin Behrman (1904–20) presided over the beginnings of these transformations. The longest-standing mayor in the city's history, Behrman oversaw the crucial infrastructural changes that enabled rapid development in the face of the staggering debts left by Reconstruction after the U.S. Civil War. Although his party operated as a political machine, Behrman's public works, including hospitals, schools, and public parks, could be associated with the civic aims of the Progressive Era. Known as "the good roads mayor," he embarked on the drainage plan so that, in his words, "Land, before worthless, became at once available for agriculture and city development."[7] Behrman oversaw the doubling of New Orleans in both space and population. His ability to mediate between elite factions and a working-class voter base paid off, both politically and directly into the city's coffers, as the assessed value of land doubled in the city between 1904 and 1920.[8] It was in this setting and in the context of these changes that the first filmmakers flocked to the city to find a new home.

FILM ECONOMY TAKE 1: SELIG

It was January 1909 when the famed film producer William Selig dispatched his best cameraman, Francis Boggs, and a "moving tableau army" composed of "twelve competent artists, several carloads of scenery, half a dozen improved and up-to-date machines, electrical appliances, to produce storm effects, etc." to New Orleans. According to a trade report at the time, the Chicagoan Selig had every intention of maintaining a "very strong producing organization" there.[9]

Selig was no stranger to the city. His company had made a series of shorts about Carnival events in 1902. Marking what may have been the first public concession to filmmakers, Selig received "special permits from the Mayor of New Orleans" to go behind the scenes of the spectacle.[10] In the interlude between the first visit in 1902 and the journey to make a studio in 1909, Selig had seeded the first major film distributor for his films in the South. The Dixie Film Company opened in New Orleans in 1907 when the owner William H. Swanson, a fellow Chicagoan, got his first loan from Selig. In an early effort to create a vertical monopoly, Dixie signed distribution contracts with a growing chain of exhibitors. In New Orleans, Dixie's local manager Herman Fichtenberg opened three movie theaters on Canal Street, seemingly ensuring that Selig's movies would always find a public screening. In 1908 Dixie became the southern hub of the Consolidated Supply Company, an exclusive licensor

FIGURE 3. Architect's photo of White City Amusement Park illuminated. From Emile Weil, H. A. Benson, and Albert Bendernagel, *Illustrations of Selected Work of Emile Weil, Architect, New Orleans, La., 1908–1928* (New York: Architectural Catalog, 1928). Permission granted by Southeastern Architectural Archive, Special Collections Division, Tulane University Libraries.

of films made by members of the Motion Picture Patents Company (MPPC). Even though Selig was included in the exclusive group of producers, the relationship with Swanson and Fichtenberg seems to have soured quickly.

The local newspaper reported that Josiah Pearce & Sons, Fichtenberg's biggest movie-theater rival, received Boggs and the rest of Selig's crew in the city in 1909. The crew immediately got to work, producing reels and establishing a local movie-industry infrastructure. Boggs borrowed office space in a Pearce theater near Canal Street. They made at least four ten-minute shorts (or four 650-foot reels). All would premiere in a Pearce theater. He leased stage space from White City Amusement Park, a public attraction in its own right. Opened in 1907, the park was designed by the noted architect Emile Weil and featured both opera and theater performances. The park's headliner attraction, its 1,500 electric lights, would undoubtedly give Boggs both an excellent setting for evening shoots and an audience already excited for his presence.[11] Boggs had created for Selig a perfect synergy between film production, exhibition, and urban leisure.

Yet within a few short months, Selig's best man closed the New Orleans studio and fled to Los Angeles, never to return. One report stated that Boggs was "not quite satisfied with the results of his stay in New Orleans and wrote to Mr. Selig about returning to Chicago." Another article attributes the California move to Selig but likewise relates that Boggs found New Orleans "not entirely satisfactory." Later accounts are more conflicted as to who made the decision, though most point to Boggs. Indeed, after Boggs's death, Selig asserted that he saw New Orleans as his "Winter quarters," and that his relocation to Hollywood came only after Boggs found the Crescent City unsatisfactory.[12]

While there is no definitive answer to the question of why Selig and Boggs decided to leave New Orleans so fast and so assuredly, after so many investments and plans, it seems probable that the answer encompasses a combination of economic and cultural reasons. From a purely industrial standpoint, Selig seems to have embroiled himself in a clash of distribution and exhibition titans in the most important southern hub for film consumption. In less than two years, Selig had allied with Swanson and Fichtenberg only to betray them. Swanson, for his part, turned on MPPC producers, attacking the cartel's membership as evidence of anti-Semitism in the industry. Selig then pursued Swanson as "one of the worst offenders in the business" in defrauding MPPC manufacturers of royalties. Swanson eventually challenged the trust in court, eventually leading to the MPPC's downfall. Meanwhile, Selig's former collaborator Fichtenberg cried foul over new MPPC licensing fees. In March 1909, the theater owner canceled Dixie's contract and organized over 250 regional theaters into the National Independent Moving Picture Alliance—a group that did not do business with Selig. By the time Boggs left New Orleans, his competitor Pearce had assumed regional management of the General Film Company and was the new national distributor for MPPC films.[13] Leaving New Orleans may simply have been an outcome of the chaos introduced by Selig himself when he had founded Dixie two years earlier. Los Angeles seemed relatively easy, even if remote, in comparison.[14]

Beyond the wars of distribution, however, there may have been other reasons that New Orleans was less "suitable" as a home for the film industry than Los Angeles. As discussed in the Introduction, Los Angeles was hardly a mecca for the labor-intensive production of a highly flammable technology. There were no self-perpetuating clusters of studios or centrifugal forces of industrial agglomeration. Selig moved operations into a defunct saloon in an isolated farming town where unpredictable earthquakes and dry, windy fire conditions tempered local boosters' claims of perfect conditions year round. All the same, Boggs may have felt more at home in his native home state of California than he did in Louisiana—and this cultural affinity for the *place* may have made the key difference.

The fact that Selig's brief but failed sojourn to establish a New Orleans film studio, and dominate distribution and exhibition in the process, escapes any cold calculus of costs and benefits suggests that cultural contexts are also important to the making of a film economy. Although it would be hard for researchers to measure film producers' level of comfort with the local scene, particularly a century later, we know that management's perception of risk is the intangible and irrational force behind all modern industrial markets.[15] For emerging cultural industries, which rely on the ability to consolidate financial support for a high-risk investment such as a film, entrepreneurs' subjective perceptions may be paramount in deciding where the home base should be located. The economic geographer Michael Storper places a high premium on face-to-face interactions and human relationships for "learning, building trust, and reducing risk" in the development of new economies based on innovations.[16] He argues that individuals' experiences of local contexts, including the price valuing of production resources and social hierarchies among the workforce, are the reasons why new industries ultimately cluster in one city but not in another. Culture, in other words, mediates business leaders' experiences of situations: "where we are matters to what we know and what we choose."[17]

Local context was surely on the minds of many filmmaking entrepreneurs other than Selig. During the entire period, from about 1909 to 1914, producers were scouring North America looking for locations to move their production operations. These manufacturers needed to expand geographically to satisfy year-round demands for increased filler films, especially between MPPC Trust members, as well as the competing needs of exhibitors in their own unique markets. The "director-unit system of production" was a mobile response to these conditions. Trust members moved *simultaneously* between Los Angeles, New Orleans, Jacksonville, San Francisco, Denver, and even Havana in search of the optimal production places. In this way, they could spread their risks around, while taking advantage of various local contexts.[18] Eventually, though, they had to make a decision in order to reap the efficiencies of proximity to each other, and then their perceptions of local contexts could be the deal breakers. At least on the surface, New Orleans and Los Angeles, as well as other cities in the South and West, offered the same economic potential for a new film economy. Each had varied locations, predictable and usually mild weather, abundant land, cheap labor, and municipal services. Each city also had its enthusiastic boosters, eager to promote the competitive advantages of the place and downplay the disadvantages. Boggs's affinity for the local context in Los Angeles over New Orleans thus had real implications—not just in seeding an economic cluster for film production, but in making Hollywood the preeminent signifier of a film economy.

When the Los Angeles boosters won out over competing cities, they succeeded in dominating the subsequent narrative of how film economies form. The region lacked people, infrastructure, and any interest from Wall Street speculators. Within five short years, business leaders went from doubting that the region was even viable for any large-scale manufacturing in 1908 to championing the region's destiny as a world business center in 1913.[19] The consolidation of a narrative that Hollywood was a natural hub for the film industry became a self-fulfilling prophecy, attracting future entrepreneurs and a workforce for an industrial cluster while marginalizing native-born populations that did not become part of the new film gentry.[20] Also perpetuated in the various films Hollywood has made about itself, the merger of Hollywood as place and industry became so totalizing as to erase the histories of other cities eligible to be film capitals in the early period, including New Orleans. There, the local context—with a cultural politics that Boggs likely found strange if not intolerable—may have been the deciding factor in why so many film crews left the city for a more "suitable" location in Southern California.

FILM ECONOMY TAKE 2: RISKS AND THE RISQUÉ

By 1912 the New Orleans film economy seemed ascendant. In addition to Selig's brief encounter, several other film producers sojourned to the city, including Howe, Lubin, Lasky, and Kalem. Each company, led by a director and crew, saw the potential in making New Orleans their future home base. Mayor Behrman welcomed them, providing public concessions to the parks and "passports" behind the police lines at parades. The *Daily Picayune* effusively praised each of the traveling companies, covering their activities with the same fanfare it gave other dignitaries who stayed in the best hotels on Canal Street. Such was the case, in particular, of Kalem president Frank Marion and his theater-actor-turned-director George LeSoir.

From his post at the upscale Hotel Grunewald, LeSoir turned a spotlight on the New Orleans waterway Bayou St. John as the perfect place for a production studio. Imagining himself moving to the site of privateer Jean Lafitte's colonial headquarters, LeSoir added that the area had everything to turn "a Lexington Avenue antique dealer . . . green with envy."[21] LeSoir met with Behrman at Pearce's opulent Trianon Theater to discuss the deal, and soon after, Marion announced the company's expansion plans. Kalem had already been producing shorts in the city before his decision. In Marion's estimation, the ideal weather, the antediluvian houses, the easy access to exhibitors and distributors, the experienced theater and thespian community, including Mary Pickford's sister, as well as "the most seductive tipple he has discovered anywhere," made New Orleans an easy choice.[22]

Yet, like Selig Polyscope before them, Kalem and the other prominent manufacturers made many films but never relocated. Lasky merged with Zukor's Famous Players, dividing their operations ultimately between Los Angeles and New York. Lubin Manufacturing returned to its original home base in Philadelphia, where it opened a massive lot and facilities in the nearby countryside. Kalem's Jacksonville and Santa Monica studios would continue to operate through the decade. And, just like Boggs before him, LeSoir left New Orleans within months of his arrival. Despite a "very profitable" experience in the city, he left the film business, returning to work in New York City theater.[23] LeSoir and others left a considerable oeuvre of films in their stead. All were shot in New Orleans but advertised and exhibited internationally. In this regard, the filmmakers who came to New Orleans found a place that was eminently filmic but industrially unreceptive.

To understand the gap between the well-publicized desires of these entrepreneurial film migrants and their inability to actualize them involves a deeper understanding of the local context for creative production. In general terms, cultural geographer Allen Scott explains that *creative production* refers less to specific industries or roles in them than to the milieu that workers share across arts-and-entertainment sectors in particular urban areas. It is through the milieu—the social environment for training and experience—that workers gain public recognition and recognize each other as *creatives*. Recognition allows access to both the resources and the pathways established through the prevailing business culture. For Scott, these pathways are most important for those trying to launch a new creative industry, as its founders will depend on the paths of established creatives in the network.[24] In other words, the development of a new film economy depends on the cultural politics of a location. In this regard, Los Angeles and New Orleans, despite sharing other external factors in favor of a film economy, could not have been more different.

While Los Angeles city leaders despaired for the lack of any industry, New Orleans city leaders saw film as a complement to more central industries and their economic agendas. Despite opposition to many of Behrman's proposals and tactics, the political consensus was that New Orleans could be a modern metropolis only by reinvesting in its traditional industrial assets. This included the technocratic development of the port and railroads to better serve what had always been leading regional industries: cotton, timber, sugar, and coffee. The vision, which required expensive infrastructural upgrades, also relied on the city expanding its tax base. The city had become heavily leveraged and embattled with local banks, which refused to supply interest on the city's liquid holdings and to extend new lines of credit.[25] Bankruptcy loomed if the city could not transform its marshy surrounds into valuable—and thus taxable—properties. Business elites valued local film production and exhibition only to the extent that it assisted these other aims.

Media campaigns for the city, as articulated by the newly formed Association of Commerce, included buying newspaper ads, seeding magazine stories, and "developing several plans for making motion pictures of New Orleans."[26] An inaugural member of the association, Pearce was both a close ally of the Behrman administration and a proponent of more locally focused film production. He had made arrangements for the filming, processing, and exhibition of industrial documentary shorts to boost Behrman's portrayal of the "progressive little city" in charge of the port.[27] The Association of Commerce organized numerous film events, such as the centennial celebration of the Battle of New Orleans, and vowed to streamline the permitting of public space for visiting film crews.[28] The association also contracted with the short-lived and Denver-based Paragon Feature Film Company (1914–16) to make several pictures intended primarily to show northern and eastern audiences of "a certain class . . . the real reconstruction that is in progress. . . . All phases of the commercial and industrial activity of the city will be brought out in the pictures. Scenes along the riverfront, at the factories, and in the parks, playgrounds, and schools, all will tell the story of the new New Orleans."[29] The fact that the company went bankrupt a year later could have impressed on some city boosters, and certainly Pearce, the importance of seeding a film-production company located in the city's bounds.

Elite New Orleanians' perspectives on the role of filmmakers as propagandists in their political economy could be deduced from local coverage of their productions in the *Daily Picayune*. Headlines of Boggs's arrival stressed that the company would add "to the Fame of the Metropolis" with pictures of the city's "historical points of interest" as well as "the City Hall, several of the big bank buildings, the Courthouse, the Parish Prison, other structures known to fame." Scenes of cotton and sugar loading at the port and views along the levee would be "calculated to give the people in the North, who know New Orleans *only by reputation,* an idea of the city's commercial importance."[30] Stressing that "all interests" would be mobilized to assist filmmakers, the paper collaborated in Behrman's opinion that film could rebrand the place by advertising the city to "thousands without access to magazines and circulars." In the same article, another traveling film exhibitor reportedly sent his director to film the 1912 Carnival as part of a campaign "advertising the South and inducing our own people to visit portions of the United States, instead of going to Europe."[31] The paper promised that the filmmakers, for their part, would be sensitive to local expectations. The *Daily Picayune* wrote that Boggs's films would be "intensely realistic and true to life in this city as the older citizens knew it before the war."[32]

The actual films that the visiting producers made, however, played into a different agenda from the ones their hosts envisioned. The city's investments in shipping and rail ironically made the location less filmic. A film-industry commentator later reminisced that "the [Selig] company was somewhat disappointed in what was offered for filming" in New Orleans. Boggs, who hoped to shoot "river-front scenes," found that the railroads now blocked any open views of the "ship loading at the port."[33] Instead, Boggs shot the stories of New Orleans he could already envision. In them, New Orleans was a place to party for the moment, not to produce durable goods for the long run. Film reels included *The Shriners' Pilgrimage to New Orleans* (1909), *Mr. Mix at the Mardi Gras* (1909), and *Four Wise Men* (1909), a comedy about four hen-pecked husbands who are "caught by their wives as they were sight-seeing through the wild revels of the 1908 Mardi Gras Carnival."[34] All of Boggs's films reproduced, in a sense, the city's burgeoning image as a tourist destination—the reputation, as noted in the Introduction, that the city itself had been promoting since the 1890s.

Similarly, LeSoir's film subjects quickly demonstrated his taste for representing New Orleans more as a cultural exception to the United States than as a vital industrial center. At first LeSoir seemed to be the perfect political propagandist. His reels of the Behrman administration's public works were screened throughout the city and were credited with the mayor's reelection, despite the opposition of "nearly all of the newspapers of New Orleans."[35] Yet his fictional works became increasingly bawdy. These titles included *The Belle of New Orleans* (1912), about a woman who elopes with a gambling French count; *Girl Strikers* (1912), staged in a tobacco factory; and *Into the Jungle* (1912), in which New Orleans was a proxy for Africa. Worse, LeSoir used the relative isolation of the bayou-based studio to complete *A Bucktown Romance* (1912), reportedly the first film in which "all of the characters being negroes" would be in blackface.[36] The sequel, *A Gent from Honduras* (1912), featured a biracial romance when the main blackface character introduces his "dusky gal" to a "Latin" lover and "now he's looking for another gal."[37] Fascinated by his idea of the place, LeSoir seemed tone deaf to his local patrons' needs or self-image, repeating instead the city's reputation in the North as a place that "stirred" desire with scandalous mixtures, from cocktails to peoples.[38] Even after their releases in exhibition venues outside the city, there are no records that any of the Pearce theaters, which held the distribution agreement with Kalem, showed these controversial films by LeSoir.

The cultural politics of film production in New Orleans had to be complicated by the inconsistencies between the internal commercial aims of the city's establishment and the external cultural meanings associated with the city, even if these contradictory messages were derived from some of the same sources. White elites drew visitors to the exotic processionals of Carnival, manufactured to memorialize their own authority, long before the earliest filmmakers flocked there. Northern publications circulated tales of voodoo and Storyville, creolism and cocktails, courtesy of their local correspondents and a fledgling industry dedicated to luring outsiders by marketing New Orleans nationally as "the city care forgot."[39] Numerous stories in the film trade magazine *Moving Picture World* stressed to readers the city's hospitality, not its hierarchies, and promised the filmmakers a warm reception, despite incipient battles of censorship elsewhere. Throughout the period, some of the same businessmen who built up the port and cultivated film producers safeguarded urban places for frivolity and vice from the onslaughts of moral reformers.[40] Given the tight networks between the civic boosters for commerce and the profiteers of libertine lifestyle consumption, the film economy was path-dependent on creatives involved in producing a cultural exceptionalism that early filmmakers could neither ignore nor embrace. During his stay on Canal Street, LeSoir was exposed to these mixed messages sent by his business hosts and the hospitality and leisure industries. He may have mistaken New Orleans's cultural marketing for the attitudes of its merchandizers, who rejected the reputation they peddled.

As if to echo the film producers' dilemmas, the Sunday literary commentator in the *Daily Picayune*, Will Branan, regularly articulated the complicated cultural politics of making a film economy in New Orleans. In often lengthy exegeses, Branan questioned whether the commercial successes of Pearce, Fichtenberg, and the other Canal Street exhibitors did not come at the expense of the culture that elite New Orleanians wanted. He regularly praised the efficiencies of the exhibitors, while dismissing "movies" as the "little sister" of theater both "legit" and "vodvil" (vaudeville).[41] With their exaggerated budgets and inflated payrolls for public relations, the film industry exploited both the culture and the cultural labor in its production locations, according to Branan. The average citizen, whom Branan named "Mr. Jones," then had no choice but to reproduce his exploitation because, as underpaid as he was, he couldn't afford the ticket for a more respectable theater production. He chided, "Is it not significant then that there has been no 'legit' theater on Canal Street since the passing of the old Grand Opera House in 1906?"[42] Combining the kind of class critique with elitist cultural mores that would do a vulgar Marxist proud, Branan attacked film production as a shell game that doubly exploited workers and consumers.

Addressed to a well-to-do audience, Branan's comments also unwittingly emphasized the ambivalence elite New Orleanians might have felt in making New Orleans a film-production hub. On one hand, the film industry had much in common with the other dominant creative sectors in the city, such as theater and performance arts. Like film, these latter industries were built on entrepreneurial ambition, hired a local workforce, and occupied a central place, both in terms of physical location and appeal to consumers. Film was one of the many amusements drawing people to spend money and time downtown. On the other hand, the film industry was a threat to these complementary sectors. Built on speculative finance and manufacturing for the lowest cost, film production could put theatrical stock companies out of business and drove down the cost of competing cultural events. Beyond this, Branan's opinions had distinctly racial undertones. In arguing that the film industry catered to the lowest common denominator, he wrote how "the lowest class of movie houses" served primarily New Orleans's large "negro population."[43] This point would be reiterated later and much more directly by Pearce himself in distinguishing between his high-class movie palaces for the city's relatively small white population and the shabby and substandard houses for everyone else.[44] In either case, the consensus of the city's elites implied that a film economy was only valuable if it focused on the cultural needs of white patrons.

The role of race relations in shaping the development of film economies has been understudied, if not completely overlooked, by historians and geographers alike; yet it is also clear that early film producers negotiated their perceptions of risk through their own sets of racial assumptions. It is unknown how the filmmakers who came to New Orleans would have reconciled their myth of an Africanized culture with the complicated racial politics there. Early-twentieth-century New Orleans saw the rise of lynchings and the increased segregation of public services at the same time that the city promoted its multiracial mingling on the street.[45] Increased production models and tight shooting schedules meant that film directors had little time after arrival to decode everyday negotiations of class, color, and bloodline.

In considering local conditions, film directors seemed to have misread the racial codes of New Orleans. Boggs, whose film scripts "were given to racial and ethnic epithets," was a racist who believed in paying his only nonwhite employee only half the wages of the lowest-paid white person. This man, whom he physically abused in public, killed Boggs in 1911, only two years after Boggs left, having found New Orleans so distasteful.[46] Could it be that Boggs was uncomfortable settling in a city with not only a nonwhite majority, but also a history of biracial unity among striking labor unions? Was it that local politicians often appeased these workers through informal and non-interventionist policies?[47] Although it may be impossible to know the answers to these questions, other directors had similar difficulties in navigating cultural differences. LeSoir's films all but ignored the race and class sensibilities of the New Orleans white elite whom Pearce sought for his clientele. Instead he created movies predominantly for a northern audience who clamored for "Negro plays" at a time when New Orleanians threatened race riots over narratives perceived as anti-southern.[48]

In perhaps the worst misjudgment of the local racial landscape, another director who arrived in New Orleans with much public acclaim, René Plaissetty of France, was reportedly the darling of the local high society until he decided to make a feature with an all-black cast. The *Moving Picture World* related the scandal of Plaissetty's disastrous plans to make a series of voodoo films using "hoodoo niggers" he procured from the city prison.[49] His refined hosts reportedly were horrified because, first, New Orleans would be the proxy setting for the Congo in the films; but also because Plaissetty planned to use forced labor. This complicated reaction to the film director, who then either ran or was run out of town, speaks to the difficulties outsiders had in fitting the local milieu for creative production. While New Orleans was officially segregated, more informal considerations of workers may have trumped certain racial divides or cast a pall over certain injustices. While elites praised the creative abilities of their esteemed guests, they wanted control over the content of their productions. Film directors had to deduce which messages local elites would like and which ones would be offensive, which must have created uncertainty for the early film crews looking to invest in the location.

Accounting for these intangibilities may also explain why Behrman and his co-hort began seeking an indigenous film-production company, one that could better assist the city's path toward modernity.

FILM ECONOMY TAKE 3: A LANDED PRODUCER

The dismantling of the MPPC, beginning in 1915, opened new opportunities for local film-economy capitalization. The local exhibition circuit was now well established. National distributors had made New Orleans a regional capital for licensing content. Pearce and Fichtenberg continued to operate the most prominent movie palaces, which were supported by local merchants advertising in their own weekly circulars. Both also had expanded into the suburbs, securing a local place to dominate leisure in the new neighborhoods. Two daily newspapers, the *Times-Picayune* and the *New Orleans Item,* each dedicated column space to motion picture news supported by the exhibitors who advertised their screening schedules. Word of the film industry's success in developing an arid and faraway Southern California spurred the wishful thinking that New Orleans could recapture what it had lost merely a few years earlier.

Prior to the Hollywood boom, few local business leaders may have fathomed that film producers could do more for New Orleans than work as propagandists of the agenda du jour. Yet it took little time before they concurred that a local film studio might boost property values in the new neighborhoods of the rapidly expanding metropolis, hence expanding the tax base for other reforms. In this respect, Pearce may have been prescient. The city's mogul of film distribution, theater exhibition, and the promoter of film production in the Association of Commerce, Pearce likely sought to land a production studio to better integrate his own film, amusement, and real estate interests. After all, he had personally brought Boggs to the White City location. Pearce also had a personal stake in Kalem's studio on the bayou, which Marion reportedly selected after an unnamed native explained the "local conditions" to him.[50] When his efforts to lure established filmmakers failed, Pearce joined an array of locals interested in developing more homegrown strategies.

In early 1915, the general manager for the Association of Commerce announced the city's first indigenous film company "composed of New Orleans men entirely and the list of stockholders includes the names of some very wealthy men."[51] A full-page story in the newspaper disabused readers of the misconception that local film production was purely publicity: "It is distinctly a business—a serious, manufacturing, money-making business. A small group of New Orleans men were shrewd enough to see it, and a close corporation was formed."[52] Company leaders estimated that their New York connections would generate $2,000 weekly in film licensing sales to theaters nationally, but 75 percent of the revenues would remain

FIGURE 4. From the *Times Picayune Magazine*, December 20, 1914, p. 3. Public domain. From Louisiana Research Collection, Special Collections Division, Tulane University Libraries.

in the city. The association boasted that the studio would lure investors from New York and Europe to the only "purely-local motion-picture manufacturing corporation in the South," becoming a valuable asset for "advertising the city and the state" and generating salaries and purchases that rank with "some of the largest manufacturing plants in the city."[53] In a subsequent headline, New Orleans would be a "Motion Picture Paradise."[54]

The company began as the Coquille Film Company, but "a week later, the company said it would release films made in the Coquille studio under the name Nola Film."[55] The unfortunate incident with the French director Plaissetty, together with a bit of legal wrangling with the backers, may have led to the sudden name change. Transferring ownership from the high-profile manager to a relatively less known member of the local elite, William J. Hannon, the company's name change was advertised as fortuitous for promoting the new film economy. Explaining to readers that Nola stood for New Orleans [N.O.], La., boosters were not too subtle in stating the allure of merging the industry with the city as a place: "The heads of business figured long on the best way to announce to the world that New Orleans is making picture films. . . . And does not 'Nola' sound like a pretty Creole girl?"[56] Within six months, the Nola Film Company had finished its studio at Bayou St. John on a tract of land owned by Dr. Louis Morey Holmes.

By the time the dream of a film economy really took hold, land speculators had already begun to cash in around Bayou St. John. The recent allocation of 1,300 acres to City Park, one of the largest urban greenways in the United States, spurred housing developers seeking white, middle-class families to relocate to a neighborhood protected by racial covenant and connected to downtown via a new streetcar line that replaced the old freight rail. Lot sales in the area across the waterway were booming in 1904 when Holmes bought an old plantation house as part of 1.8 undeveloped acres for $6,000. Nearby, planners eyed the area around Holmes's house as an upscale leisure destination, announcing the construction of a $15,000 Country Club House to connect City Park, two boating clubs, and another neighboring park. When the clubhouse plan tanked, the liquidating agents hoped the purchaser might find a new use for the structure, perhaps as a "moving picture studio." After LeSoir abandoned his dreams of a film studio next door, Holmes began leasing the plantation house and its adjacent grazing land to the Nola Film Company for $100 a month; he announced publicly that he would sell the entire plot for the inflated price of $20,000.[57]

While Holmes focused on his local property, Hannon promoted the value of the film studio's place nationally. Trade-magazine reports claimed that New Orleans residents could take "much civic pride" in the fact that Nola Film would be advertising "that picturesque location to the world."[58] Nola contracted two cameramen from established film studios Pathé and William Fox and gathered a cast of seasoned thespians from well-regarded stock companies. National ads promoted Nola's rental facilities and production capacities, including a 4,320-square-foot

FIGURE 5. Postcard of the Country Club at City Park, 1907. From Louisiana Research Collection, Special Collections Division, Tulane University Libraries.

FIGURE 6. Advertisement in the *Moving Picture World*, vol. 30, October 21, 1916, p. 456. Public domain. Retrieved from the Media History Digital Library, http://mediahistoryproject.org/.

ventilated glass studio to let in natural light while protecting the production from the natural elements. The public relations campaign seemed to work to the degree that film producers continued to flock to the city, including representatives for Fox, Essanay, and Lasky. Selig even expressed renewed interest in a New Orleans studio. With a familiar set of entreaties, Nola and the city repeatedly stressed to outsiders New Orleans's diverse shooting locations, Old World charm, and New World amenities. Behrman relayed that his city was the most hospitable for studios and would be offering incentives to create mutual advantages for filmmakers and for New Orleans.[59] In theory, Nola represented everything local elites could ask for in terms of propaganda, industrial development, and expanding the tax base with highly valued properties.

Nola also seemed to fit easily into the city's political and economic culture. In his role at the Association of Commerce, Coquille's original leader was the main representative for local commercial leaders and between the city and the labor unions. A former newspaper reporter himself, he also knew the writers and publishers who would report on the company's evolution. Nola's founding member Hannon shared his predecessor's milieu as an association member, lawyer, real estate investor, and esteemed yacht-club member. Working as insiders in the local context, Nola Film worked hard to respond to Branan's claims that the film industry was not as respectable as other creative arts. Hannon's father stepped out of his law practice both to become the scenario editor for Nola Film and to lend more credibility to the entire industry by publishing an extended essay titled "The Photodrama: Its Place among the Fine Arts" (1915).[60] Reproduced in the local newspaper, the essay anticipated auteurist film criticism and studies of the industry for an accepting middle-class consumer: "Ultimately, he [Hannon Sr.] understood that film is art as well as commerce."[61]

Unlike the visiting film directors who frequented the city, Nola Film pursued a path to cultivate its growth through local synergies with newspapers, local businesses, and labor. The *Times-Picayune* was particularly enthusiastic about the film economy, reprinting a company press release stating the need for interindustry ties between film and newspapers. Adding their stamp of approval, the *Times-Picayune* opined:

> There is no disguising the fact there is an air of subdued excitement in all sections of the local motion picture field, and those who watch the signs closest are preparing for a break of any sort. They are about in the position of a man who lives along the Mississippi levees at the present time. They are not possessed of any particular fear, yet they are not absolutely comfortable [. . .] not because business is bad, but because it has been so good, that it is all balled up.[62]

In subsequent articles, the *Times-Picayune* and competing daily the *Item* touted the high quality both of Nola's films and of the local entertainment professionals and residents who donated their time, talent, and homes for film production.

Nola Film also became a poster child for the short-lived M-I-N-O campaign to choose products "Made-in-New-Orleans." The company stressed their investment in the local economy, both in terms of the studio and in their weekly payroll expenditures, which they estimated to be $700 for a budding film labor force. The company further availed itself to local businesses to advertise their "plant, factory or store" with their "expert cameramen" and "highly trained artists." In return for

PEOPLE OF GOOD OLD NEW ORLEANS

Here, at last, is your opportunity to see

Photoplays Made in New Orleans

Local Capital, Local Talent Have Made

NOLA FILMS

Which Are Produced in the Nola Studio on Bayou St. John

You've seen thousands of California-made photoplays, thousands of New York, New Jersey and Florida-made photoplays. Once in a while you've seen photoplays with a few scenes taken in New Orleans. But never before have you had a chance to see produced and finished wholly in New Orleans—real honest-to-goodness

M-I-N-O PRODUCTS

The photoplay industry is the Fifth in volume in the world. It pays enormous salaries. The photoplay industry put Los Angeles on the map—after New Orleans had thrown away the opportunity to get the pioneer Western studio, Selig.

Consider what this means to New Orleans.

Now New Orleans has a first-class film studio—and is making first-class film plays. If you want these to continue—if you want other big producers to come here to stay—then foster the productions of our own home town—Encourage M-I-N-O products. See NOLA FILMS and tell your friends to see them at

COLUMBIA THEATER

CANAL AND BURGUNDY

Where they will be shown for the first time for

BEGINNING EASTER SUNDAY

APRIL 23rd

Big Features and Comedies Will Be Shown

NOLA FILM COMPANY

1347 MOSS STREET

FIGURE 7. Advertisement from the *Times Picayune,* April 16, 1916, p. C-13. Public domain. From Louisiana Research Collection, Special Collections Division, Tulane University Libraries.

Nola's investment in the city, the M-I-N-O campaign asked residents to see their films, because "Ninety percent of [Nola's] expenditures go to New Orleans people and only two percent of its income comes from the same source."[63] From production to consumption, the campaigners argued that Nola was to anchor a chain of other film and amusement businesses in the city, and chided those who "had thrown away the opportunity to get the pioneer Western studio Selig" before "the photoplay industry put Los Angeles on the map."[64]

In the end, however, Nola Film was not durable as the keystone for a local film-economy cluster. Selig came and left once again, as did the rest of the interested parties. As would become evident in other cities that were trying to seed a film economy at this time, civic boosterism may have incentivized local production and driven up property values, but it could never sustain an entire industrial sector. Even if the location of the first entrepreneur is completely random, other entrepreneurs must follow, along with their financial investors, technology suppliers, and connectors to other support networks.[65] By 1915 the owners of New York's nickelodeons, such as Zukor, Laemmle, Fox, Mayer, and Warner Brothers, had already migrated to Los Angeles. New producers also came from theater and newspapers in the Big Apple, and Lasky started the first American film education program at Columbia University. Together, these people took with them and maintained their organic ties to big-city money, resources, and personnel. Location mattered in creating a film economy in Southern California, but not in helping directors choose scenic studio sites or finding local business partners. Instead, Hollywood built a powerful publicity machine that, through its connections to the New York newspapers, universities, and creative sectors, drove Wall Street speculation and bank credit lines.[66] While Los Angeles reveled in hosting an American industry to invest in, New Orleans doubled down in making sure the film industry would keep its networks local and its culture provincial.

In the process of building its local stature among businesses, Nola Film lost its connections to national distributors and financiers that would invest in a film cluster, which led, eventually, to local failure. Although Coquille had initially strong ties to Pearce, Nola's films ended up screening at minor independent theaters around town. Ultimately, Hannon was unable to ink a deal for national exhibition, or even for regional distribution through the exchanges based in New Orleans. Without preorders for guaranteed distribution, the company was wholly dependent on its local stockholders to foot the bills. Only eighteen months after their premiere movie, the company made society films, capturing weddings and special events. Desperate for outside recognition, Hannon signed what would appear to be a mock distribution contract with a fly-by-night company in New York City, just before declaring bankruptcy in 1916.[67] In short, Nola Film had become too dependent on local conditions.

Even bankruptcy did not break New Orleans's dreams of creating a film economy and envisioning itself as a future movie center. In seeking to boost tourism as a local industry for the first time, a newly reorganized Association of Commerce reported in 1918 that the organization "has also been very active in exploiting New Orleans and in attracting moving picture producers to this city."[68] Association representatives returned from New York with illusions that producers there would relocate to New Orleans for its "lighting, setting, as well as labor."[69] No longer on the periphery of the city's strategic aims, Hannon made one last attempt to leverage the film studio as a tool for economic development.

FILM ECONOMY TAKE 4: A DIAMOND IN THE ROUGH

Like Coquille and Nola Film before it, the Diamond Film Company promised to make New Orleans a film-production capital. This time, however, Hannon's appeal to local investors rested solely on film commerce and not on film art. With an initial stock offering of $200,000 at $10 a share, the Diamond Film Company promised buyers it would be a cash cow. Hannon claimed that the company had already contracted its principal employees and signed a distribution deal with the General Film Company worth $250,000 annually. Echoing the Progressive vision of the Behrman administration and a M-I-N-O plea for goods made at home, Diamond's success would be "of advantage to the city from a business as well as a sentimental point of view, for the outlays of salaries and supplies would all go into the coffers of local people."[70] The company's investor handbook reprinted Horatio Alger stories about those in New York and Chicago who had made their fortune in film manufacturing. Diamond repurposed stories in the *Times-Picayune* about Nola Film to evidence its sure future and the ability of New Orleans to rival Los Angeles, which, according to Diamond, had become *over*crowded with studios. These rationales aside, the majority of the handbook's pages were dedicated to glossy photos of the Bayou St. John studio facilities that Nola Film had already constructed: "Here we have one of the best equipped plants in all America, ON WHICH WE DO NOT OWE A DOLLAR."[71]

In fact, Hannon probably began Diamond already in the red, and the production facilities were far from finished. The former Nola Film had boasted that its laboratories were "the best equipped in the South" but then had to send its film stock north; a newspaper report at the time waffled that the studio "*could* be turned into a splendid and complete producing plant."[72] Further, the photos printed in the Diamond investor handbook did not display any actual equipment for filmmaking or film processing. When a building contractor sued Hannon personally for not settling his bills, Hannon countersued—first the contractor, for libel; and second the Diamond board of directors, for nonpayment of debt. The amount of the contractor's debt was approximately the same amount Nola Film was said to have

FIGURE 8. Photograph in Diamond Film Company, *Filmland: The Kingdom of Fabulous Fortunes* (New Orleans: Schumert-Warfield-Watson, 1917). Public domain. From Louisiana Research Collection, Special Collections Division, Tulane University Libraries.

invested in its studio years earlier. Whatever material assets Diamond Film had were liquidated at a bankruptcy auction a year after its well-promoted launch. The studio was to be demolished and sold for scrap lumber.[73]

This is not to say that Diamond never intended to be profitable, but that their margins would not be tied to film production. Rather, Diamond likely was developed to leverage aid to a variety of regional property schemes. Diamond's publicly named board of directors comprised a group of business and real estate speculators. The board president launched the Diamond Theater, a suburban exhibitor in another nearby and growing neighborhood. Together with his theater co-owner and four of the seven remaining board members, the men founded the Interstate Oil, Gas, and Development Company, a sham drilling operation located in the swamps southeast of the city. They drove up Interstate's value by purchasing the surrounding, useless land—probably using the funds of Diamond stock buyers— and reselling them back to the company at an inflated price. Board members essentially manipulated stock investors and then paid themselves through real estate deals. Interstate's stock purchasers eventually won more than $100,000 in a court case against the con artists with Diamond.[74]

The receivership hearings and liquidation of Diamond's assets coincided with Interstate's expansion and indictment. In what would seem an effort to avoid linking the two companies publicly, Diamond reshuffled its board at the last minute. The remaining members profited handsomely again on land value. The soon-to-be demolished studio was appraised at $20,000, no doubt based on the land's sale price nearly five years earlier. Diamond's penny-stock buyers never received a dime back on their investment. The lawyer and notary who oversaw the proceedings opened his own real estate firm soon after.[75]

Holmes also profited from Diamond's failure by contributing to a property bubble in the neighborhood. Stories in the newspaper had already characterized the bayou as a "favorite and wonderful setting for movie action," but the film studio was built to communicate the power of a new film economy.[76] The glass building loomed over the well-traversed waterway in front, and Diamond erected a sign on the house so large that it was unmistakably advertising the industry. From the summer of 1915 through the spring of 1916, realty ads for the studio-adjacent land prominently promoted the studio next door. When Diamond succeeded Nola Film, the area became even more marketable. The negotiated sale of the Country Club property to a suburban developer boosted land values for all of Bayou St. John. "There is dollars-and-cents value in beauty," said the developer. Although he never got the full asking price, Holmes parceled and sold his lots, including the transformed plantation house, for three times their original value in 1919. He moved to Baton Rouge as developers quickly settled the once fallow land.[77]

While Diamond was not the only fraudulent film company during the silent era, its tragic trajectory should be instructive as to the real commodities in a film economy. First, land speculation was ultimately more profitable than the films themselves. It is questionable whether Diamond even planned to release their films beyond the theater owned by the board president. Hannon had promised to complete one picture a week but in fact never managed a true feature. The "Big Weekly News" reels of "interesting events and travel from all over the universe" offered such small-scale attractions as a women's war-registration drive and a Tulane football game, and these screened only at the Diamond Theater. The company announced a comedy series, but no record survives of its completion. Diamond's schedule actually cited producers who had been dispatched from other companies, had already made their films, and had left the city.[78]

The seeming lack of profitable production points to a second lesson about film economies: the real beneficiaries of the local film companies, from Coquille to Diamond, were the studio owners, not the film workers. The fledgling film economy did not create generous payrolls or revive the floundering theater stock companies. Local exhibitors were already marked as shoddy employers; projectionists complained publicly and led strikes for better conditions.[79] On the production side, Plaissetty and Hannon managed to contract only one actor of national repute and to train only one veritable film star. While the former actor had been reduced to playing vaudeville in New Orleans, the latter actress left town to become the acclaimed starlet Leatrice Joy. Beyond this, the directors frequently used their family as talent. Hannon's father, the defender of film art listed as Nola Film's scenario editor, played a female lead in drag in the company's first release. Plaissetty's three-year-old daughter played children's parts. Those most qualified to become part of a local creative network for film felt they had to either make their names in Los Angeles first or maintain their real career in New Orleans's independent theater scene. All along, the local newspapers continued to relay to their readers the dream of being discovered; one even hosted a popularity contest to identify the paper's "prettiest" subscribers for a local movie shoot. The winner of the vote was guaranteed to become a star, in Hollywood.[80] These two lessons about property and labor in making a film economy seem relevant today.

AND SCENE? RESTAGING THE TEMPORAL IMPACTS OF FILM ECONOMIES

The history of New Orleans's early film production is allegorical to the extent that cities and film studios are still involved in a dance of mutual attraction. The independents working for small- and medium-size firms that comprise the vast majority of Hollywood film production in the past thirty years hold much in common with the mobile and itinerant filmmakers of a century ago.[81] Both groups seek to reduce their risks in deciding where to produce for the short term and where to locate for the long run. Those risk perceptions are as much personal and political as rational and economic. To succeed, film producers must weigh the importance of direct incentives alongside cheap resources, such as land and labor, which can be made more cost efficient when they are shared with other creative sectors. Their dance partners, the government and business officials who have sought film production since the silent era, also share common cause with those of today. Beyond city branding and the seeming synergies with tourism, city leaders must decide who are meant to be the biggest beneficiaries of the film economy. While the creation of local circuits of production, distribution, and consumption may generate good will and stimulate a temporary market, creating a sustainable film economy ultimately lies in satisfying the needs of financiers and venture capitalists first. At the local level, city representatives must wrestle with the thorny moral questions of resourcing a film economy that so easily benefits the most propertied elites. Wrapped in the cold cost-benefit analyses of what makes film economies run, then, are the stories of real people navigating these difficult ethical choices.

These intangible factors help explain why New Orleans's film economy so frequently failed to replace Hollywood's, and why so many runaway film regions continue to run after the Hollywood dream. Much has already been made of the success of Los Angeles's boosters, but that success is more symbolic of film production than a direct index to it. Even in Hollywood's earliest stages, its boosters protected their place's brand as studios meanwhile sought cheaper rents in nearby Culver City and Burbank. In doing so, they propped up real estate values and safeguarded the glamorous consumer lifestyle associated with the place. The real work of film production happened elsewhere. To this day, Culver City has not reaped the benefits of an iconic name, even though it is now where more studios are headquartered and where more film and television workers go to earn their wages.[82]

Today, New Orleans uses the moniker "Hollywood South," having forgotten the history of its own ignominious efforts, first to lure filmmakers and then to seed an entire industry. The name also has its allure, conjuring the aura of glitz and glamour around a place more easily recognized as the "birthplace of jazz," the "city care forgot," and "the Big Easy." These traditional titles have had their merit in attracting film producers looking to pursue their own pleasures, which was the main idea behind those who heralded the need for each city to chase down "the creative class."[83] Like LeSoir, however, they may find that the perfect cocktail does not make a sustainable new creative sector; and just like the M-I-N-O boosters of yesteryear, the city may find that the price of achieving the temporary local symbolic capital is not worth the cost. "It was cruel irony that the urban boosters' very striving for economic success [in the early 1900s] only deepened their region's economic inferiority," writes the urban historian David Goldfield about a number of short-term competitive strategies that southern cities, including New Orleans, have pursued in order to achieve more recognition.[84] Whether by promoting the cheapest labor, the malleability of the urban environment, or tax incentives that favor the rich and steal services from the poor, boosters have unwittingly helped concentrate wealth at the top of the social hierarchy and exploit those at the bottom. Worse, the strategies are inherently risky. Some cities will lose to others in their race to the bottom.

And Hollywood as an industry and a place continues to be relatively durable. Fewer films are shot on location there, but the creation of new wealth and the maintenance of some of the highest property values in the world have continued unabated in the center for the film industry. New Orleans business schemers, from the respected exhibitor Pearce to the sleazy exploiter Hannon, knew this in their efforts to use the film industry to expand the city's boundaries and its property values. In time, each of the new neighborhoods created in New Orleans in the 1910s and 1920s had its own cinema and linked to the Canal Street leisure district via streetcar. What the planners failed to achieve, however, was an equitable way to distribute their profits among city residents, particularly those redlined out of the neighborhoods on the march. In this way, Diamond's backers did not just prey on those who dreamt of a film economy, but they also validated the racist and classist property divides that the film industry itself embraced and marketed to middle-class whites. The recurrent scandals around the current film tax policy shine a light on the greed and fraud potential that surrounds a policy based on government nonintervention, spiking land values, and naive investors who believe that if they help build it, Hollywood will not only come, but stay and flourish.[85] Yet the sensational coverage of insider trading, sham productions, and embezzlement are only minor elements in a long-term strategy that further stratifies the haves and have-nots.

Hollywood South

Structural to Visceral Reorganizations of Space

At first glance, everything about Hollywood South seems mobile, if not virtual. Unlike Hollywood, a place rooted originally in a nexus of studios and today radiating out to a network of joint business partners in the Greater Los Angeles Area, Hollywood South seemingly has no such physical markers. There are no actual home offices and only a few dedicated physical locations in the form of sound stages and production houses. The only central managing offices might be the government offices in Baton Rouge charged with both the industry's sustenance and its oversight. Whereas Hollywood emerged from the settling of filmmakers in a location, Hollywood South first existed on paper, the result of proactive government staffers, industry lobbyists, and elected representatives. As described in the Prologue, the incentives for film production are themselves mobile, passing between producers, financiers, brokers, and buyers before resting on a final balance sheet. Even the legislation authorizing the incentives for film production is a moving target, the result of strategic revisions and last-minute addenda in every budget cycle.

The stated objective of the policy itself has been to attract location-based film production, itself a seemingly ephemeral and weightless endeavor that leaves no footprints behind. As described in the Introduction, Louisiana's law was a forerunner in the United States in creating expedient efficiencies for film producers looking to reduce their risk and for regional governments looking to stake claims to a new economic engine. Yet others have used cultural policies to engineer a film economy. Press reports at different historical moments have hailed a new "Hollywood South" located in Texas, Florida, various Australian cities, Cape Town, and the Argentinian pampas before Louisiana claimed the mantle. Today, Georgia threatens to steal the title away, though it was Hollywood South in the late-1990s.[1]

Within Louisiana's borders, New Orleans dominates location shooting, though the city loses some business to the studio facilities at the opposite end of the state in Shreveport and in the middle of the state in Baton Rouge. The shoots themselves can last a day or a week, but seldom more than a month on the same set. Television series may use space recurrently, but that too can change from setting to setting and season to season. At different moments, location shooting seems to be happening everywhere in New Orleans, but nowhere in particular. "This industry doesn't put down roots," opined the *City Business News* in 2005. "It moves to the most advantageous tax climate possible. Right now that setting is Louisiana."[2]

These expressions of political and economic power remake space. Much like sports franchises and high-tech firms, film companies can use their regional perks to move operations anywhere.[3] The disintegration of the big studio monopolies over all aspects of the industry left a competitive market in production, the aspect of filmmaking in which investors take the most economic risk, and producers thus scramble to do more with less. Easier technologies and transportation have helped close the distances between different stages of production and their often itinerant labor forces. In the era of competitive public film subsidies, space is a tangible trade that can lure film projects and tempt workers to stay long term.

Contrary to the metaphors of rootless mobility, Hollywood South not only put down roots, but also partnered in transforming the way it feels to move around in New Orleans. Mapping the physical locations where films are shot and where their temporary crews cluster helps us visualize the patterns of spatial uses in Hollywood South, including the tight and expedient relationships between film production, tourism, and gentrification. These patterns follow historical industrial paths and a trajectory of internal colonialism that left the city more unequal after Hurricane Katrina. These patterns also have gotten under the skin, interrupting mobility around the city and creating the unsettling feeling that urban space under these private–public partnerships belongs to someone else. This transformation has been a sentient experience in my own wanderings around the city, reinforcing where I can go and how. I track these paths, not only as a counterpoint to the myth of rootlessness and weightlessness, but also in showing how the driving mythology of the film economy relies on the "differentiated mobility" of those social groups who can direct the movement of people in space—and those ultimately kept in stasis or excluded from those spaces.[4]

COLONIAL AMBITIONS OVER THE LAND

While Hollywood South may have no brick-and-mortar edifices to embody its existence, the reorganization of space in New Orleans is produced by the shared structures, or homologies, between the film economy launched in 2002 and the tourism economy that preceded it by half a century. With their colonial aspirations, elites in both industries found common cause in the post-Katrina moment to reshape the urban landscape for their own profit.

The word *colonialism* refers to the domination, containment, and control of a social group within a territory. In this sense, New Orleans has a colonial power structure in that elites have maintained their wealth and status on the backs of a population kept in poverty and in spaces demarked by race and class. The social justice activist and scholar K. Animashaun Ducre argued after Katrina that the flood revealed nationally the internal colonialism that had enforced racialized spaces in the city since its founding. While this dynamic has not been unique to New Orleans, the city compensates with stories of its own exceptionalism. As I explained in the Introduction, these stories are marketed primarily through the tourism industry.

Since World War II, New Orleans's establishment moved from its focus on shipping, banking, warehousing, and insurance to develop tourism. In doing so, the city ceded both public space and history to the commercial needs of hoteliers, developers, and preservationists dedicated to framing the city's history as romantic creole charm rather than contemporary colonial inequality. For just like shipping before it, "the greatest profits from tourism found their way into rather few hands."[5] In spatial terms, the epicenter of the tourism industry is the conjoining areas of the French Quarter and the Central Business District (CBD). Whereas the former neighborhood displays the iconography and stories of the city's heritage, the latter contains the financial and physical infrastructure for managing the industry and its flows of visitors throughout the year. The abundant service jobs needed to support tourism have been occupied by a nonwhite underclass that can nary afford to rest, much less settle, in the French Quarter and the CBD, except under heavy surveillance. Meanwhile, the vast workforce for the city's leading industry relies on public subsidies that enable them to live and travel between peripheral neighborhoods and the downtown core. This tourism geography—today managed by the publicly funded but privately operated New Orleans Metropolitan Convention & Visitors Bureau and the New Orleans Tourism Marketing Corporation (NOTMC)—is an effect of the internal colonial structures that maintain de facto class segregation despite de jure racial integration.[6]

It was the power brokers in these structures who infamously looked to eliminate public goods through the mechanisms of privatization after Katrina. Dubbed the "exclusionist movement" by the well-connected director of the Southern Institute for Education and Research, the private profiteering from the redistribution of public goods up the social ladder in post-Katrina New Orleans has been well documented in journalistic accounts and scholarly research.[7] Without any public input, city elites together with planning experts began answering the profane question of *where* should be rebuilt. They tried to "deal with the city's blighted neighborhoods by engineering them off the map."[8] From the shuttering of public housing projects and the end of the only hospital for indigent care, to the efforts to turn public schools into privately managed charters and working-class neighborhoods into green space: "New Orleans as a city increasingly divided between those who it had been purposely rebuilt for and those who it has manifestly attempted to exclude," in the words of historian and social critic Thomas J. Adams.[9]

How the film economy dovetails and supports this upward redistribution of wealth speaks to the colonial tendencies within the film industry itself. Much like the tourism industry, Hollywood has always aspired to spatial domination. When the sociologist Leo Rosten called Hollywood "the movie colony" in 1941, he was not merely describing the well-accepted merger of a geographic region with a dominant industry; he was also examining the concentration of economic and cultural power in that space. Indeed, the centralization of film studios, together with their agglomeration of related and servicing firms, had made for a colonial-like social system. At the top, Rosten documented a group of no more than 250 people who led the industry in terms of both salary and social capital. They were a nervous bunch, in constant pursuit of more property and public approbation. The rest of the industry's workers fell into line in support of these goals, presumably leaving everyone else at the margins, both of the local social structure and of the Hollywood cultural milieu. In what might be called a rather blithe application of the totality of colonial dynamics, Rosten revealed the ways in which film work and film workers produced the land they occupied.[10]

While Hollywood continues to dominate the spatial flows in Southern California, the global expansion of film production might be better described as imperial rather than colonial. The short-term, project-based orientation of Hollywood since the 1960s underwrote the contracting out of film production "as the major studios gradually adopted the business practices common in the independent sector."[11] Today, the hub controls the deployment and movement of an array of contracted film companies and their subcontracted service providers via telecommunications and travel infrastructures, guaranteeing maximum flexibility in mining profits elsewhere. Film scholar John T. Caldwell calls Hollywood "the para-industry," culling the reference from the infamous regimens of paramilitary contractors, such as Blackwater, which have occupied territories in the name of their employers.[12] Importantly, occupation is not simply economic, but also cultural. Each contracted unit is a "profit-driven hermeneutical enterprise," complete with its own self-theorizing rationales and reflective analyses to justify its position in the larger field of operations.[13] These justifications form their own unique narratives, including countless ways that the industry enters places, establishes control, and then leaves when those places no longer suit the contractor's mission. In other words, Hollywood's colonial ambitions are less a unified force of domination than a peripatetic system of rhizomes, with each unit of the network spreading quickly and taking control of existing structures in its own fashion.

FIGURE 9. Spatial impacts of location shooting on an Uptown residential neighborhood.
Photo by Aline Maia, reproduced with permission.

The symbiosis of development aims between Hollywood film producers and
Louisiana government officials can be traced to a small revision in the state tax
code in 1990. In it, the code articulated Hollywood's role in a new economy: "It
is hereby found and determined that the natural beauty, diverse topography, and
architectural heritage of the state, the wilderness qualities and ecological regimen
of its scenic rivers system, and the profusion of subtropical plants and wildlife provide a variety of excellent settings from which the motion picture industry might
choose a location for filming a motion picture or television program, and together
with those natural settings, the availability of labor, materials, climate, and hospitality of its peoples has been instrumental in the filming of several successful
motion pictures."[14] The implication was evident in the wording: the film industry
needs locations, and Louisiana has them. Added to this, Louisiana would sweeten
the pot with accommodating weather, workers, and studio-ready warehouses to
create a film-friendly destination. In return, the code continued, "The multiplier
effect of the infusion of capital resulting from the filming of a motion picture or
television program serves to stimulate economic activity beyond that *immediately
apparent on the film set*."[15] The tax code envisioned a virtuous exchange between

the producers and the consumers of a unique place beyond the set, one in which the place is only enhanced by the film crew's presence.

The balancing act between film friendliness for production companies and multiplier impacts for state officials was, in itself, nothing new. Several states in the 1980s and 1990s had almost identical language in their tax codes, usually meaning a repeal of lodging or sales taxes in return for motion picture production.[16] These state policies were cribbed from production incentive policies crafted abroad, creating an international pitch tournament to attract Hollywood production. As the competition got more intense, with a wider range of places bidding for Hollywood films, the policy crafters had to make places more malleable to the needs of the producers. This happened at local, regional, and national levels of governance. What began as the purview of film commissions now extended into massive, coordinated, and ongoing "placemaking" strategies between government and infrastructure agencies, commercial businesses and their associations, representative citizen and neighborhood groups, and public service (e.g., safety, health, and transportation) providers. Film friendliness has involved shaping both locations and locals "to build or develop local capability and capacity to host and service inbound production, to educate local communities about the benefits of filmmaking, and to market a place to filmmakers as a 'pro-film,' low-risk production destination."[17] In Louisiana, these capacities to host, serve, and market had already been captured by the tourism industry.

While the policies originally aimed to develop the most depressed areas of west Louisiana, it was quickly apparent that New Orleans would be able to best capitalize on the multiplication of film-production impacts within its own tourism infrastructure. In the three decades prior to the first film tax incentives, the city pinned its economic future to the expansion and promotion of its local hospitality industries. Fueled by a short-lived oil boom that attracted thousands of new taxpayers to settle in middle-class neighborhoods, a new urban business elite used public funds to spur developments to lure and service tourists with recently constructed venues for entertainment, lodging, and leisure. The result, according to historian Mark Souther, was a "creole Disneyland" that promised to satisfy the needs of increasingly affluent visitors, whether oil executives in from Houston or suburban families, white and black.[18] What this meant, both for tourism and for film investors, was that the city would modify the place to suit the desired buyers.

Within a decade, the draw of the state's regionally distinctive spaces as proposed in the original policy had slipped into a grab bag of resources that Louisiana had on offer for film studios. The 2002 film incentive policy, introduced as Title 47 of the tax code, offered film producers with budgets over $300,000 credits for using "*substantial* Louisiana *content.*"[19] In an unconventional interpretation of the word, *content* as referred to by the law could mean locations, labor, or both. In addition, without defining *substantial,* the new program funded producers who did much of the studio production work, and all of the post-production work, out-of-state while cashing in on the entire budget for the project in-state. After this loophole was closed by later revisions of the policy, the political salience of the state's physical locations in spurring industry investment declined.

Instead, film policy followed in the footsteps of a tourism industry eager to make spaces respond to market demand. In 2003, legislators deleted wording that would mandate that the newly formed Louisiana Film and Video Commission market "desirable locations within the state for the production of motion pictures" or "siting or location filming." Instead, the commission would broadly promote "key economic, social, and cultural benefits of basing film and television production in Louisiana."[20] With this, Louisiana entered the regional competition for presenting its space as a relatively open slate for film investors. Couched in a win–win language for economic, cultural, and social development, the policy incentivized the creation of new spaces over preservation of existing spaces. Tax credits were extended to cover infrastructural development, including nearly any construction project used in or for production purposes.[21] The definition of "Louisiana labor" was also expanded to encompass any employee who had moved to the state for more than six months in a year, an incentive designed to motivate studios to relocate their payroll workers inside state boundaries.[22] The only references to production activities in physical locations around the state were embedded in a public relations agenda for local governments still trying to compete with New Orleans.[23]

By 2015, after multiple rounds of tinkering with the efforts to be film friendly, the colonial needs of the tourism industry and the film industry had converged. Beneath a veneer suggesting that both industries use but do not abuse space, each works to make the entire city responsive to their needs. A critical report on the film economy in 2012 conceded that the policy would never seed a stable film hub with physical locations that would rival the power of the major studio complexes.[24] Rather, the state in general, and New Orleans in particular, offered film companies the equivalent of an all-you-can-eat buffet of malleable locations, complete with flexible labor and services at the ready. The para-industry, by this logic, needed to roam freely. And New Orleans needed to court the film industry as it did tourists, with place-based adaptations and spatial redistributions. No longer conceived as a Disneyland, which would exclude social groups from the city center and whitewash their history, film companies and tourism prefer a city that can be an available canvas for meaning-making. Media scholar Helen Morgan Parmett prefers the term "Disneyomatics" to describe the ways these industries compel every neighborhood to compete for attention and subsidy, whether public or private, to show their worthiness.[25] The competition, framed as open and inclusive, operates at a structural deficit for citizens who cannot sell their neighborhood as a distinct place. With the full support of the city, the logic of Disneyomatics has redrawn the map of New Orleans, letting Hollywood South occupy land, identify its value, and modify it to its own greatest benefit.

HOLLYWOOD SOUTH AND THE INVISIBLE INFRASTRUCTURES OF PRIVATIZED SPACE

The struggle to evidence and produce value as a justification for public investment has been one of the primary ways that Hollywood South participated in the all-out spatial warfare waged in the city after Katrina. Public space is a political manifestation of a territory, which governs its uses through zoning, permitting, and enforcement. In cultural terms, public spaces are sites of struggles over modernity, between stakeholders in different visions of an urban community.[26] With much of the population displaced from their homes, planners and developers—many of whom were involved in the construction of the city's tourism infrastructure—envisioned the urban blueprint as a blank slate that could better be capitalized. As they headlined in the local newspaper, "Hardest-Hit Areas Must Prove Viability," a message accompanied by an influx of multinational subcontractors to control the process of assessing land and property values.[27] Even as local residents raged against them, these third-party assessments led to a refashioning of the entire city. Under the twin banners of "renewal" and "rebirth," the City of New Orleans embraced "new privatization strategies" that emphasized public–private partnerships as a form of operational best practice for the distribution of public goods and stressed entrepreneurialism over the uses for public space.[28] In these struggles, Hollywood South seemed inculpable, hidden beneath its own shiny aura and mythologies of weightless mobility.

Privatization, however, is a structural and visceral process, one that gets under the skin as public space responds to political and market pressures. The sociologist Richard Sennett plotted the experience of public space as one that has been increasingly individualized. On this continuum of the past three centuries, modern urbanites gradually rejected public space as a zone of active engagement with strangers, and instead became traveling spectators in the public. Industrialization encouraged people to treat public space as a mere passageway to the more important zones of work and family. What citizens witnessed in public space enabled them to reflect more on their private life.[29] Such experience, ever more personalized and detached from the experiences of others, confronted another set of social relations under neoliberal governance and postindustrial restructuring. Not confined to New Orleans, the federal abdication of funding of public goods and institutions is what precipitated the new social contracts between local governments and private companies to offset the shortages. Broadly speaking, these transformations have disrupted people's expectations of physical space once again.

The changing governance and geography of post-Katrina New Orleans owes much to Hollywood South. The 2002 incentive policy positioned film companies, developers, and the city to be convenient collaborators in returning properties to the market through short-term rentals, purchases, and resale. These broad interventions put the private life of citizens into direct conversation with the forces of privatization in their daily lives. The influx of film workers and their preferred spaces for location shooting not only affected the neighborhoods where these citizens live and work and the public places where they play, but also contributed to the privatized ways in which citizens have learned to move through space in their city. Each of these impacts can be examined in turn as we look at the ways Hollywood South has reorganized space in New Orleans.

1. Location, Location, Location

Hollywood South defines its own spatial uses by its variety of locational shooting spaces. Regional marketing campaigns aimed at film executives and producers have alternately sold the state as offering either distinctive places or generic spaces that can be remade into "Anywhere U.S.A."[30] The City of New Orleans boasts both. For more than a century, the tourism industry has packaged the French Quarter as America's most unique and historically Old World place, while the mix of skyscrapers and early-modern buildings in the CBD could stand in for nearly any contemporary U.S. city. Location scouts frequently come to New Orleans in search of both of these types of spaces to fit film scripts, and New Orleans offers spaces to suit their needs.

The New Orleans Office of Film and Video (NOOFV) assists with location shooting directly by recommending spaces and the scouts who can vouch for their film-friendliness. The office streamlines public permitting for the use of roads, bridges, streetcars, police, or any other city personnel in a location shoot. Office staff even meet with neighborhood associations and mediate any potential conflicts "to keep New Orleans film friendly" for producers and residents alike.[31] These services are free, funded through the state's tourism funds. The permits themselves can be attained for a nominal fee.

City service providers, including police, fire, and medical personnel, are subcontracted through each agency's procedures. When budgets are lean, the reorientation of these services to be more entrepreneurial means they are less available to the general population. In 2011 a federal investigation found that film studios were the largest clients for public police details, calling it "an aorta of corruption" that funneled kickbacks to assigning officers. Paid to secure movie sets from outsiders—tourists, fans, and random residents alike—police details for film became lucrative ways to boost the notoriously low salaries of people on the force. The film economy was so profitable to police officers that after Katrina, the department established its own "check-writing service" to process requests more efficiently.[32] In these ways,

FIGURE 10. Signs directing workers, including police details, to a neighborhood film-production location. Photo by Vicki Mayer.

spaces and their public caretakers in the city are for sale; they are part of a market that few people can access in such a privileged way.

In 2013, fewer than a dozen location scouts were the primary buyers in this market for the lion's share of the major film productions receiving tax credits. They selected the spaces and assessed their value in relation to their projects' bottom lines. Interviews with five location scouts showed that they all knew each other.[33] They had developed track records with the studios and the city, moving to New Orleans just after the passage of the 2002 incentives policy led to major film shoots in two residential neighborhoods.[34] Despite their expertise, however, they remained a rather mobile labor force, traveling between the states competing for locational dominance with incentives. Union records from 2007 to 2012 show that as many as eighteen location scouts were registered with the Local 478, but in that time, ten had arrived in state only in the past five years, and four others had moved out of state in exchange.[35]

In contrast to the workers, the spatial patterns of actual shooting locations in the city have been relatively stable. A study of city permits filed with the city's Office of Traffic and Transportation reveals how film companies' use of public space is concentrated geographically. Over four years (from January 1, 2007, to December 31, 2010), film personnel filed more than eight hundred permits for productions that would receive state tax credits. Some of the permits allowed crews to park equipment on public roads for indoor shoots, while others sanctioned the closure of entire streets or blocks for outdoor shoots. Using a calculated metric for

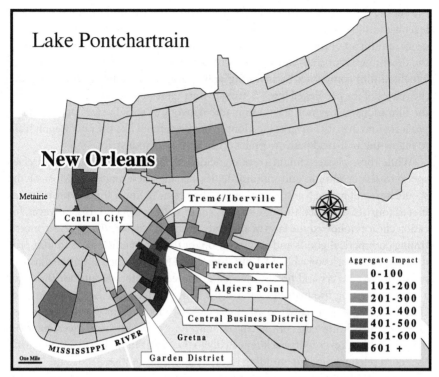

MAP 1. Aggregate impacts of location filming activities by major Hollywood productions on urban public space in New Orleans, 2007–2010.

the duration and intensity of public-space use, a map of the city visually demonstrates the areas with the highest and lowest concentrations of film production in public spaces.[36]

Far from the myth of its own mobility, film location shooting makes the highest use of the two neighborhoods already assessed with the highest commercial value, before and after the storm. As outlined earlier in this chapter, the French Quarter and the CBD have been the epicenter of the tourism industry since the end of World War II. Before that, as shown in chapter 1, they were the hub of the city's shipping, banking, and other commercial interests, with the highest concentration of leisure and entertainment options for locals and visitors alike. After Katrina, many rebuilding efforts began in these two neighborhoods, despite the fact that neither of them sustained as much damage as the rest of the city. Using a combination of state, city, and federal funds, private investors coveted this area as an upgraded destination for professionals to live and play in. Together with millions in state and federal aid, Mercedes Benz sponsored the luxury refurbishment of the Superdome for billionaire Tom Benson, while the city used federal money and leveraged millions in its own debt to finance a streetcar line between the Superdome, a number of renovated upscale hotels, and the French Quarter. By "feeding the downtown monster," in the words of the geographer David Harvey, the city benefited film companies by investing public monies to better enable and equip the spaces of the privileged few.[37] Setting their trailers in precisely the same spaces, the film industry has not been a nomadic network of social actors or innovative pioneers into the city's diverse locations. It has been more like the next wagon train to follow the well-trod paths worn by other dominant industries.

While these clusters might seem coincidental, the location scouts themselves spoke to the economic and cultural logics driving these patterns. Most of the scouts were not native New Orleanians, so they came to know the downtown areas first as tourists, and then through the city's film staffers. Beyond this, however, location choices followed the laws of agglomeration. The city's dedication to concentrating commercial goods and services brought their own efficiencies to film production. Film trucks on a blocked city street could be positioned simultaneously in proximity to caterers and hotels, the well-groomed park for an outdoor shot, and a bevy of working fire hydrants for a scene with pyrotechnics. As one scout said, "I'm not going to hopscotch to another neighborhood if I got that in one place." Together, their knowledge of the city, enhanced by public–private investments in infrastructure, drew scouts back repeatedly to the places they already knew. Citing the social relationships surrounding location shooting, another scout said, "It's really about familiarity and knowing where I can park, who are the property owners, who are all the players involved, where I can get all of my support parking, and all of my support space." By pulling crews into familiar locations, scouts benefited from prior knowledge of the place (including who is authorized to give space and facilities) and thus saved time managing the locations during production.

In the end, film location shooting replicated the symbolic assets of those places where they clustered. Old World and New, the French Quarter and the CBD looked as different as could be, but together their geography symbolized the "upper-class lifestyles that dominate in Hollywood films," as a scout said, continuing: "Most films aren't going for the gritty real-world experience. They're going for a little Hollywood beautiful picture. And most directors [. . .] want their pictures to look good no matter what the story is. So when I say 'polished' and even if we get away from the iconic restaurants. . . . You still are creating an upscale imaginary world that these people lived in that we'd paid money to go see." In other words, to locate anywhere else would gamble that the production space no longer syncs with the class assumptions embedded in most Hollywood film and television scripts.

Meanwhile, the permits map shows most of the city as a territory untouched by film production. Virtually no film crews purchased space or contracted public services on the city's eastern and western sides or in the swath of working-class neighborhoods that cut through the middle of the city.[38] These areas included the neighborhoods hardest hit by flooding, which, arguably, would have benefited most from an infusion of public spending and support. Yet these neighborhoods were transformed too, showing that film locations may symbolize a wealthy life-style on the screen, but filmmakers create wealthy locations when they use public money to buy property on the cheap.

2. Movin' On Up

As if taking a page from the playbook of the Nola Film Company in 1914, Hollywood producer Peter Hoffman and his New Orleans-based wife purchased a dilapidated, pre–Civil War mansion in 2007 for $1.7 million to start a film studio. Working with the Hoffmans was Michael Arata, a New Orleans lawyer and bit actor with such enviable roles as "man with piña colada." The studio project was a "real estate success story," according to the local newspaper, turning an eyesore on the urban skyline into an example of film-economy entrepreneurialism. Both Arata, whose wife was deputy mayor of the city, and the Hoffmans, who owned a prominent restaurant and tourist attraction in the French Quarter, were well con-nected to the city's business elite and to Hollywood studios. The group claimed that $13 million was needed to renovate the house, 90 percent of which would be paid through tax credits from state film and city historic-preservation funds. Echoing local boosters for a silent film studio, Peter Hoffman argued that the city itself would draw producers to finish their films there, rather than sending them back to Los Angeles after the location shoot. "They can do the complete sound of a $200 million picture right here," he said. "Rather than going back to L.A. and do-ing it, they can stay and be happy. They can walk over to Frenchmen [street music clubs]. They can go over to the French Quarter." He and Arata were convicted in 2014 of fraudulently receiving $1.1 million of their film tax credits, which they had sold already for a handsome profit in 2009. Ultimately, the renovated Whann-Bohn house would attract film-producer tourism. Situated close to the city's music and entertainment scene, the new owners operate a pricey bed-and-breakfast for visiting "Film and Entertainment industry tradespeople [looking] for an unforget-table New Orleans experience."[39]

The case of the Whann-Bohn house would be an outlier if it were not part of a larger strategy within "creative economy" policy. Proselytizers for film economies tout the use of public funds to return "undervalued properties" to the real estate market, where they can find new economic life for private investors. By offloading their risk onto the public, the investors can look to profit by building production infrastructure and "loft-style living" accommodations for film personnel.[40] When film economies fizzle, as the Michigan one did in 2012, the public is left holding the bag. A bankrupted film studio in Pontiac, Michigan, used $70 million in tax incen-tives to renovate an old General Motors facility, leaving years of holes in the city's budget and the state pension fund to cover the project's bond debt.[41] Still, these projects have been a boon to real estate speculators who have scoured the abundant New Orleans inventory of abandoned warehouses, factories, and nineteenth-century estates for easy renovation dollars.

The Whann-Bohn project, along with hundreds of other development ideas, relied on an infrastructural film tax credit, which was hatched in 2004 as a separate program from the film-production credit. Justified as a key to sustaining the film economy, the infrastructure tax credit was more generous at the time than the production credit, allowing 15 percent *on top of* the regular 25 percent credit awarded to productions. Although a lobbyist later told me this was an error of poor wording in the bill, the definition of infrastructure included "any moveable and immoveable property and equipment related thereto, or any other facility which supports and is a necessary component of" film, television, and video production and post-production.[42] The unintended consequence of the policy led to a flood of proposals for a series of construction projects only loosely related to film production, causing the legislation in the following session to specify that hotels and golf courses would not be covered under the program. These scandals precipitated the sunset of the policy at the close of 2008, but investors have continued to cash in tax credits on projects that were certified before the deadline. According to the state's own auditing report, Louisiana gave $15.3 million in tax credits to support film infrastructure in 2010, for example; and this amount was bolstered with other state-subsidized projects to support infrastructure for sound recording and live performances.[43]

Among the projects that went forward was the city's main film studio space, Second Line Stages. The owner and developer Susan Brennan acquired the fire-damaged and decayed warehouse near the port in 1998 with an eye to making high-end condos. After sitting on the land, however, film infrastructure tax credits became more appealing. In 2009, Brennan and her partners decided to create a gold-plated venture, combining tax-credit programs to create the first LEED-certified environmental studio complex in the country. Using $14 million in infrastructure tax credits, the team then secured $10 million in federal new-market tax credits and more than $3.3 million in federal, state, and city historic-preservation tax credits for, presumably, its old buildings. Although Second Line's owners claimed that their lofty principles would give them a competitive advantage in booking "eco-friendly" entertainment executives, the studio has rarely been booked full-time by film projects. Between the three sound stages, a screening theater, and commercial offices, Second Line occupies 150,000 square feet in an impoverished and relatively desolate part of the inner city, where the shrinking footprint of the port abuts a housing project that was razed, post-Katrina, to make way for mixed-income housing. Prior to the hurricane, a quarter of the residents in the studio neighborhood lived below the poverty line; the nearby housing project offered 1,510 public units. In 2015, the mixed-income neighborhood had 182 public units while property values soared in the adjacent Lower Garden District. Second Line has returned its gifts to the public in the form of educational programs for at-risk youth, apprenticeship programs, and safety and security initiatives, but it only staffs ten employees.[44]

The vast economic disparity between those who get public subsidy through the film economy and the vast majority of working-class people who do not is nowhere more evident than in housing, where gentrification has transformed entire neighborhoods. In 2012, the Cité Européenne du Cinema was part of the city's plans to lure well-heeled Parisians to the "troubled" lower-class neighborhood of Saint-Denis through a filmmaking center, art galleries, and boho cultural tourism.[45] Recommendations for New Orleans involved coordinating the efforts of the regional development agency Greater New Orleans, Inc., the businesses represented by the Downtown Development District, the utility Entergy, and the Mayor's Office of Recovery and Development Administration to pinpoint the city's disaster recovery grants to places best suited for creative industry growth. In partnerships with local universities, land developers, and the year-long festival industry, advocates of the new privatization claimed that the city would see economic rebirth in the development of "livable communities" when an in-migration of younger, highly educated workers repopulated areas marred by high poverty and crime rates—a theory that the boosters called a "people-centered approach" with no sense of irony.[46]

Another map of the city shows the neighborhoods where a cross section of middle-class film-production workers lived in New Orleans from 2007 to 2012.[47] Members of the International Alliance of Theatrical Stage Employees (IATSE) are among the rank and file who receive steady work from the tax incentives. Producers of major-budget productions have to hire union workers before contracting with outsiders. Louisiana IATSE 478 membership has grown by 900 percent since 2003—even if, at 1,300 members in 2015, the local is tiny compared to those in California and New York. They also earn and pay a bit less than their counterparts in other regions, owing to the different cost of living in the Big Easy compared to the Big Apple or SoCal.[48]

While it would be not only impossible but unfair to blame gentrification on 1,300 individuals, the footprint of their housing choices mirrors the broader ones advocated in creative economy policies. As pointed to on the map, Bywater, Mid-City, and the Marigny have been hives of gentrification in the city, with rental and housing prices exploding. In Bywater alone, where nearly 40 percent of the population lived below the poverty line in 2000, around 20 percent did in 2010. "The declining poverty rate does not speak to some miraculous redistribution of wealth to working-class families, but rather to their forced exit amid a corresponding influx of high-income residents," writes Meghan French-Marcelin, a planning and policy historian. The market for flipped homes, which has been among the highest in the

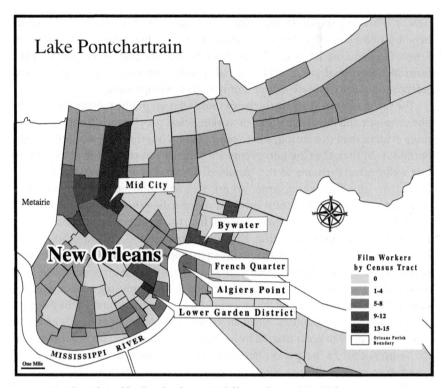

MAP 2. Residential neighborhoods of unionized film workers in New Orleans, 2007–2012.

nation even during the mortgage crisis, is due in part to the technically skilled film workers looking for other projects between formal employment gigs. These areas have also received disproportionate amounts of federal aid to rebuild mixed- and multi-use housing complexes with only a fraction of their available units designated as "affordable," and those too cost much more than before.[49]

This trend would likely be replicated if the data included the thousands of film workers who come to New Orleans for a shoot, some of whom decide to buy their own acreage. A newspaper audit of a sample of local film payrolls found that the vast majority of middle-class film workers come to the city from out of state.[50] Featured on websites such as Air BnB, VRBO, and Craig's List, the short-term housing market in New Orleans caters to mobile professionals willing to spend more than $250 per night.[51] For some at the very apex of the production hierarchy who return frequently to the city, it is often cheaper to simply buy in and take their pick of the relatively underpriced mansions that are a steal in a variety of senses. The history of film producers who declare residency outside of Southern California in order to reduce their property taxes reflects a standard operating procedure among Hollywood's elite since at least the 1950s.[52] New Orleans newspaper coverage of celebrity home buyers tout their rootedness to the city, even though their properties are rarely occupied by them. As with the native workforce, many of these rentals and part-time residents end up in the same neighborhoods affected by high gentrification. In the end, rebuilding *did* produce the sort of gap-toothed pattern of empty or infrequently occupied houses that residents feared—the "jack o' lantern effect"—except that instead of a patchwork of poor homes, the city now has a patchwork of unaffordable ones.[53]

The results are visibly evident to locals. Where dive bars and corner stores used to abound, craft cocktail bars and upscale coffeehouses predominate. The growth of eateries in the city from 800 to 1,400 in the five years after Katrina has been attributed to the influx of film crews feeding off their tax incentives.[54] Alongside these privately owned businesses, the city has crowed about public block grants used to build local food markets and green spaces, complete with new festival stages and industrial details repurposed as art. In a city with a minimum wage under eight dollars an hour and service workers struggling to get by, the pursuit of the creative class is expressed as fancy lifestyle consumption rather than encouragement of production or of guaranteed safeguards for those working in production.[55] Hollywood South walks the same paths even as it denies its own footprints.

3. Following the Signs of Privatization

Film shoots and crew housing are visible, material manifestations of the privatization of public space, but Hollywood South has also affected New Orleanians' ability to move through these physical spaces. Much of the city's iconic public culture involves traveling through the neighborhoods. The sudden transformation of ordinary space in the service of kinetic rituals and events—from second-line parades to jazz funerals, from impromptu street performances to block parties—has been celebrated in the soundbite stories of New Orleans's exceptionalism. Scholars have framed these public movements as resistant to the dominant ways in which their practitioners are kept in place, physically and metaphorically, in daily life.[56] Yet, ordinarily, the way space *feels* can seem rather mundane: New Orleanians have to go to work—and, in the local vernacular, "make the groceries"—just like people do anywhere else. In these everyday acts, movement through public space is a series of social contracts whereby "the experience of the whole is determined by the intactness of the constitutive parts."[57]

This mobility was rerouted after Katrina. The flooding of black neighborhoods, where much of the celebrated "mobile escapism" occurs, forced those who remained to determine which traditions would survive—often based on their viability for tourism, according to music historian Bruce Raeburn.[58] Transportation was upended too, affecting everyone's ability to get places, particularly the working class. Many of the regular bus lines that had traversed the city ended. Workers from across the Mississippi River who depended on public ferries to get to their jobs found that service was intermittent, closed one time for nearly a month. The gleaming streetcar line in the CBD led to the cancellation of bus services there, resulting in a steep decline in ridership of both. In contrast, film companies have found that iconic streetcars, ferries, and even bridges can easily be hired and monopolized.[59]

Perhaps nothing has shown how Hollywood South directs movement more than its signs. Affixed to telephone poles, the location-filming signs are two to three square feet, monochromatic (usually in blue or yellow), and decorated with acronyms and arrows. They are more sturdy and standardized than the usual "garage sale" or "queen mattress for sale" signs around town, but their placement implies a similar short temporality. They are generally found on the way somewhere else, for example on street corners and in entryways to parking lots or public buildings. Such spaces are what the anthropologist Marc Augé classically called "non-places," places where mobile users are encouraged to plug in and pass through.[60] The signs are impossible not to see, though some people may try to ignore them. They are part of the urban texture of the city in that they enter the sentient feeling of being located in a space, at that moment, directing actions and movement through a geography.[61]

Signs have always had a particularly special role in communicating to urban denizens. In 1928, the social critic Walter Benjamin suggested that we all should read the modern city as we wander through it; in turn, the city communicates back its gestalt meaning as if we are following a one-way sign. Following the arrow, he wrote, the critic maps the urban experience on the basis of various things one encounters on the street.[62] Yet film signs are not like advertisements or other "legible, local, 'friendly' emblems of economic power," in the words of sociologist Sharon Zukin.[63] Most of the signs are acronyms or have undecipherable phrases, like teases for a treasure hunt for "Fallen Angel," "Patriots," or whatever a "Looper" is. For example, "BC" on one sign stood for "base camp," which usually means a field or parking lot holding an encampment of trucks, trailers, and heavy equipment. Most references are more specific to the project itself. MB meant the film *Memphis Beat*. FNN was "Fee Nah Nay," the name of the local LLC for the production of *Treme*. When the temporary placards have legible phrases, they point passengers cryptically in a direction toward "Common Law" or, more confusingly, "Home." In a city in which so many people already have questioned the law and the politics of homecoming, could it be that these signs are slyly touting the film economy as the answer to residents' problems? Moreover, what do the film signs want people to do in those times and spaces?

In contrast to the film signs, New Orleanians made signs that have been far more legible in the post-Katrina landscape. In the early aftermath, homemade signs responded to those authorities and their subcontracted workers who had

FIGURES 11–14. Filming location signs are ubiquitous but speak in code. All photos by Vicki Mayer.

claimed imminent domain in enterting and seizing their residences. Some of these signs were not so subtly spray-painted on the sides of abandoned refrigerators tossed out with their rotting contents. Locals soon grew accustomed to fashioning

FIGURE 15. "Thee Broadmoor Sinkhole." Photo by Bart Everson (http://barteverson.com), reproduced with permission.

their own decorative street signs to direct officials where citizens lived and needed assistance. They hand-penned signs to hail utility workers to broken power lines after Hurricane Isaac left the majority of the city in darkness in 2012. Neighborhoods that competed for public spending used dark humor to remind the city of its spending priorities. Potholes have sported welcoming placards for city employees to visit, likening the gaping sinkholes to tourist attractions, such as the Grand Canyon or mystery caverns. When the city sponsored an international public arts exposition as an official attraction in 2008, a series of handmade signs appeared to tell readers, "You Might Be Wrong." Later associated with the expo itself, the signs drew the elite and culture vultures alike into debates about citizens' mutual responsibility and/or arrogance in the city's recovery efforts.

Unlike that debate, film-production signs close off public dialogue, directing their messages more internally. They make liminality a daily experience, posits Zukin, by disorienting readers with ambiguous messages during a time of economic restructuring.[64] To the local citizens, it quickly becomes apparent that these messages are not directed at them. The signs do not hail one to consume or come closer, to engage or react in any way. Rather, they simply announce that these non-places are spaces of production, where the hidden labor of the film industry becomes manifest and visible.[65] If anything, savvy travelers learn to move away from the directions pointed in the film signs because that is where public space is owned, for the time being, by someone else. The signs thus break those small social contracts about which public spaces we can move in or wander through. One only has to witness the rerouting of commuters trying to avoid the sometimes dense maze of filming locations to understand that these signs have a pedagogic effect over time. They teach that city space does not belong to all citizens equally.

HOLLYWOOD SOUTH'S STAR MAPS AND TOURIST TRAPS

Striving for a creative economy through mechanisms of privatization, New Orleans in a quick decade became a whiter and more affluent city with fewer spaces dedicated to housing, educating, serving, or protecting the underclass that still struggled to find living wages in the tourism economy.[66] Much like the tourism economy, the film economy increasingly, and through incremental policy changes, sought to make the land and its residents serve the needs of the most connected producers and the most affluent consumers.

The city's film office is financed through the New Orleans Office of Tourism. This mutuality is by design. It harks back to the first city permits that were granted to the visiting moving-picture crews in order to promote official Carnival festivities, as described in chapter 1. In the era of global Hollywood production, major film projects have been tied to regional planners' dreams of place-based tourism since at least the 1980s, when new film commissions sought projects that would enhance the "popular perceptions of a place."[67] At a time of incentives that were relatively modest compared to those of today, such as a hotel tax rebate, the film officials hoped that tourism would be a cumulative effect of prolonged and positive media exposure of the place over the long term. Tourism studies gave evidence that the language used in film stories could imbue local architecture with a romanticism that drew visitors long after the film wrapped. Die-hard fans could make pilgrimages to film sites, spending money in return for the chance to engage with a familiar space, revisit a remembered scene, or to simply give tribute to the power that a media story has held in their lives.[68]

Tourism operates in a push-pull dynamic with film production. The city office charged with promoting film projects and giving fans access to knowledge about shooting locations and schedules is usually the same one that has to then assist the production crews to secure the space, keeping crews in and everyone else out. By mediating these flows, the city can hope to capitalize on the same space by asking satisfied movie studios to assist in promoting it. Local officials hope that a blockbuster film will be the gift that keeps giving through movie clips or star cameos in tourism campaigns. To this end, NOTMC decided to issue a tourism app for New Orleans in 2013. Called GO NOLA, the download, currently supported with the help of actors John Goodman and Wendell Pierce, is meant to allow users to "take your pick of celebrity-narrated walking tours of famous New Orleans neighborhoods, each with a unique archive of historical documents and photographs."[69]

Media scholars Susan Ward and Tom O'Regan have likened film personnel in Brisbane, Australia, to long-stay business tourists, a characterization that fits New Orleans's own Hollywood-moneyed class.[70] The buyers of the Whann-Bohn house, for example, may have used public money to build film-production infrastructure, but a glance at reviews on the vacation rental site VBRO by a group of fifteen who came for Mardi Gras confirmed what I already knew: that movie-industry investors had reconfigured urban space to be one of their own personal playgrounds. "I've been to some of the best restaurants in my entire life," one director raved after coming to New Orleans in 2008. "I've heard some of the best music on the street with 70-year-old guys who are better than any other musician I've seen in my life. And every weekend's a festival. I will come back as visitor in addition to as a movie producer." The director added that he came close to buying a house because "if you're going to a city to shoot a movie, you do have days off. You have your family with you sometimes, and this is a pretty great city to spend time in." In 2016, the director's review was repurposed, on a quasi-public economic development website, as one of the selling points for using media tax breaks as a "creative catalyst."[71]

Ironically, when media executives decide to stay, they tend to live in neighborhoods that strictly regulate film production or keep it out altogether. The Garden District, which is home to a number of Hollywood Southerners, cracked down on filming simply by limiting shooting hours and days per year and requiring a $500 daily "contribution" to neighborhood association coffers. Other prestigious communities in the city enjoy relative freedom from major studio projects through their homeowners' associations, increasingly secured by residents' private guards. By levying their own supplemental taxes, the rich have effectively created their own exclusive zoning rules for the occupancy and use of public spaces in those parts of the city. Other neighborhoods have no such luxury. Not only has the explosion of festivals and cultural events since Katrina perpetuated the image of a public culture for sale, but these increasingly unexceptional events compete with film crews eager to find locations in the same areas. Residents have been blindsided by their neighbors letting their houses to the industry without public discussion or input. For example, one multiseason television series paid the chairman of the Uptown Neighborhood Triangle Association to rent his home, inconveniencing neighbors and attendees of a nearby elementary school who had already suffered the elimination of busing services. When about forty residents filed a petition with the city to stop the company's heavy use of public roads and its noise pollution, the spokesperson for NOOFV dismissed them, putting the onus on each neighborhood to

FIGURE 16. A filming location in the Garden District, where some of Hollywood South's elite reside but where production activities are restricted. Photo by Vicki Mayer.

decide how much exposure to the film economy is "tolerable." A few gripers, she explained, should not be allowed to overshadow the silent "thousands of residents in the city who support the film industry."[72] In other words, the media production elite is welcome to regulate their own exposure to the impacts of the film economy, while everyone else must be complicit.

In the epicenters of location shoots and festivals, the tourism industry compounds residents' inability to regulate the presence of film production in their own neighborhoods. Unlike a construction site, film-production space will not be improved for the public after its use. To the contrary, when the crews leave a street or corner, they are supposed to restore it to its original state, potholes and all. Yet the production still leaves traces in memory (even in non-places) that can be used commercially, such as for branding a new place or selling a film tour. In Toronto, another favorite destination for runaway films, the local film commission has overseen the reconstruction of downtown to look so much like the New York City skyline that new housing construction projects have adopted the names of this faux geography, including Soho, Manhattan, and the NY Towers—the latter meant as clever wordplay on North York and New York. Similarly, a study of local Toronto business owners in the Distillery District revealed they had located there for its historical association—not with distilling, but with contemporary film shooting. These changes to a place can become permanent when the filmic versions of the place become more economically viable than actual history. "If visibility is a concern for Toronto, then arguably the city is rendered less visible through these representations than if none had been made at all," argues urban studies and media scholar Aurora Wallace. Unlike in Toronto, however, film-production branding and tourism in New Orleans competes with the already hyper-visible cultural places in the city. Here, businesses have had to be creative in mapping new meanings onto spaces that have been used to portray "anywhere U.S.A."

Exemplifying these tensions over place branding, New Orleans Film Tours runs a seemingly lean operation out of a van owned and driven by former film worker Jonathan Ray.[73] Although there have been walking and bicycle tours that have capitalized on film locations in the city, New Orleans Film Tours seems to be the first and longest-running outfit dedicated to telling the story of Hollywood South. Ray got the idea for the business after he broke his arm on his first major shoot after working his way through a variety of unpaid assistantships. Laid up at home, he watched a lot of movies, including *The Curious Case of Benjamin Button* (2008), *Interview with the Vampire* (1994), *JFK* (1991), and *Easy Rider* (1969). All were located in New Orleans. He took his epiphany and his entrepreneurial pitch to NOOFV in 2010, and it was show time. What was striking about the film tour, though, was not how many movies had been filmed locally, but how few had been set there. Most of the contemporary movies shot in New Orleans had nothing to do with its distinctive spaces. This presented some challenges for Ray. When he pulled up to a nondescript parking-garage door, he directed visitors to seatback TV monitors where a *Dukes of Hazzard* (2005) car chase began with the breaking down of that door. Similarly, Ray drove the streets of CBD while referencing their roles as streets in Chicago (*The Mechanic*, 2011), Pakistan (*GI Joe*, 2009), and Panama (*Contraband*, 2012). In fact, nearly all of the post-2002 oeuvre in the tour was just average city space: street corners and open plazas, a tattoo parlor and the aquarium, under a bridge and inside a warehouse. Ray punctuated each stop with the same bucolic economic data found in the local newspapers and promoted by city and state boosters. Yet he was no shill. "You used to go film places because you wanted to show that location. Now we don't even get the benefit of showing the city in the movies we do make."

The Hollywood South of the policymakers, urban planners, and corporate executives is a projected vision of a new regionalism, founded on a subsidized industry that will use the marketplace to reverse a century and a half of unequal social relations. Proponents of this vision for Louisiana claimed that entertainment industries, including film, new media, and theater, held "the prospect for rapid export-based economic growth, high-wage employment, clean and eco-friendly conditions, and tourism promotion."[74] They imagined what the social theorist

Michel Foucault called "heterotopias," spaces that do not seem to have a fixed location or time coordinates, which nevertheless become containers for a society's hopes and dreams, as well as its anxieties and fears. Asking us to envision the uncharted geography surrounding a boat that has set sail, Foucault argued, we can only imagine what a spatial heterotopia is like for the real people located there. It is a space of projection on, and juxtaposition with, what seems to be "a place without a place."[75]

The problem is that Hollywood South has used space in ways that reproduce social inequalities. Locational occupation has countered citizens' mobility, and gentrification has displaced those who were most in need of public assistance after the storm. The film economy bolsters the worst features of the tourism economy by focusing on high-end consumption rather than sustainable production. Hollywood South may be a heterotopia, but we must remember that even imagined places are located in real spaces. Even the boat in Foucault's example must have space to move in and through. It must have public goods, such as air and water. It must be governed and must direct others within their borders. The problem with the heterotopic Hollywood South is that it seems more real than the people who happen to occupy the same spaces.[76]

The Place of *Treme* in the Film Economy

Love and Labor for Hollywood South

New Orleans is about the story. And it's about embracing the story. I think that's what you are looking for is how do you embrace the story. Everyone sees what they want out of Treme.

CONTRACTOR, MALE, AGE 38

Over the course of my research into the New Orleans film economy, one television series seemed to dominate my discussions with other people about Hollywood South. Though the title *Treme* (2010–13) refers to a single neighborhood, the HBO program was a valentine to the entire city, according to its auteur David Simon. In particular, Simon and his creative team showered their love on fellow cultural producers in the city: the writers, the musicians, the chefs, those who performed cultural rituals in the city, and their enthusiasts. Charting the stories of these proxies for "creative economy" workers after Katrina, the series heavily promoted New Orleans as an irreplaceable part of the United States with a unique and worthy culture. It ended with an abridged fourth season after it failed to attract sustained national interest, from either pay-TV subscribers or television critics. Locally, however, no other film or television program did as much to represent New Orleans as a special place—one under threat and in need of defenders.

In terms of the contemporary film economy, *Treme* was exceptional. The fact that producers touted the program as one made about and for New Orleans replicated the public rhetoric of filmmakers and their boosters as described in chapter 1. Unlike other high-profile films shot during the same period, such as *Green Lantern* (2010) or *Dallas Buyers Club* (2013), in which the city was simply a backlot, *Treme* was one of the few projects not only set in New Orleans but also created with the city at the center of the narrative. Simon and cocreator Eric Overmyer said they had planned to do a program about musicians in New Orleans before

FIGURE 17. Eric Overmyer, on a panel exploring the literary nature of *Treme* at a Tulane University event, October 28, 2010. Photo by Sally Asher, Tulane University.

Katrina, but then reframed the concept around themes of urban recovery and redemption in the flooding's aftermath. "This show will be a way of making a visual argument that cities matter," Simon said.[1] From its beginnings, the producers established a moral basis for local expenditures, hires, and philanthropy as integral to the production project.

At the same time, *Treme* was entrenched in the same tendencies as every other major Hollywood production incentivized after 2002. Producers' spending morality was thus supplemented by state tax credits, which at the time equaled approximately one-third of HBO's investment, with an extra 5 percent for local hires. The project's LLC, Fee Nah Nay, certified about $7.5 million in expenditures for the pilot alone in 2009; this figure ballooned to over $40 million for the rest of the first season. Like other productions, as detailed in chapter 2, much of that money was spent on payroll and housing for crew coming in from outside the city; nearly $400,000 went to hotels, accommodations, and per diem for them alone. Out of the total certified budget, the city recaptured less than 1 percent of the state's money in the forms of public space permits and police security details. In return, *Treme* in the first two seasons used more than 10 percent of the *total* public space used for *all* film location shooting from 2007 to 2010.[2] Like the framing of New Orleans in relation to other American cities, the program was framed as both the exception and the archetype of all runaway productions. It would be impossible to understand Hollywood South without addressing this production and how residents felt about it.

Treme was written, shot, and aired during a time when many residents in New Orleans were at the crossroads between hopeful recovery and what was known as Katrina fatigue, "a type of exhaustion that can only come with the feelings of sheer hopelessness over the loss of a life one will never get back."[3] This liminal state, according to medical anthropologist Vincanne Adams, was aggravated by the unreliable and unaccountable response of government at all levels in helping residents return to their homes. The private outsourcing of federal and state disaster relief alongside the local privatization strategies for new development "made trauma feel normal and made the 'normal' that people once knew feel like an imagined dream."[4] Meanwhile, the city had embraced the film economy as a central strategy in its recovery–transformation. For residents struggling for ways to navigate and narrate the "new" normal of life in New Orleans, *Treme* was one of the few media texts that personally hailed those who felt fatigue and loss to "Wrap your troubles in dreams, and dream your troubles away."

Indeed, that was the title of the *Treme* episode I watched with the individual whose insight opens this chapter. The title quotes a popular tune penned to deflect attention away from the impacts of the Great Depression; yet it might as well have described the uncanny zeitgeist in the backyard where this contractor's friends gathered weekly to watch the show about post-disaster New Orleans projected on the side of his own damaged house. I came there looking for the reasons why people loved *Treme*, how it reflected the city's political economy, and what they were dedicating to the series' success despite their own conditions. For, despite my critiques of the film economy, this multigenerational New Orleanian reminded me that I also longed for catharsis—a way to embrace the story of a place that felt like home—despite all the ways the film economy itself made me uneasy. This chapter focuses on the ways *Treme* helped many viewers construct their sense of New Orleans as home, even as its production became an alibi for the film economy's roles in historical and spatial displacement.

AN ARCHIVE OF STORIES ABOUT OUR COMMUNITY AND OURSELVES

Reflecting on the city's recent past, Simon aptly compared the contested nature of personal memories and official histories in writing about New Orleans to that of a diaspora. Paralleling his own lineage in a Jewish community that argues each "point, counter-point, and counter-counter-point" of its own formation, New Orleanians are defined by a struggle over their identities. According to him, "Every shard of your civic history is balanced precariously on the head of two dozen different bundles of personal memory, family history and political argument."[5] These rifts between memories and histories became public during group viewing events, on message boards and social media, and in the sociable conversations that make up local coffeehouse culture. The program thus became one site among many in the post-Katrina city in which the "struggles of distribution and recognition are played out" in an imagined space that political theorists call the "public sphere."[6] By talking about *Treme,* viewers talked about New Orleans, its symbolic boundaries and members, as well as the civic rules that bound them to the city.

I became familiar with these discussions as an insider and outsider to these times and spaces. I had lived seven years in the city when *Treme* began airing. I knew the stories being recounted on the screen weekly and was personally embedded in the networks of people working on and watching it. Working from rather traditional sociological objectives to foster demographic diversity and objective neutrality, I launched a reception study in 2010 to capture a random sample of sixteen interviewees whose voices represented different social groups in the city: black, white, creole; working-, middle-, and upper-class; men and women; Uptown and Eastside. I attended many public screenings, which gave some local residents access to the pay-TV program. After I was invited to speak on the program in a public forum, however, it became undeniable that I too was a participant in this local circuit of production and consumption.

During broadcast of the next two seasons, I treated *Treme* as a kind of "homework," a way of bridging my private life and my public work world to understand more deeply why so many people around me were so drawn to this one show.[7] I attended screenings at friends' houses and organized focus groups in my own. Undoubtedly, these groups were less representative of the entire city than the first-season interviewees had been; in particular, they were whiter and more middle class. Yet they debated and offered diverse opinions of *Treme's* roles as quality entertainment, as a "bard" for the city's recovery, and as a model production in the local film economy. They also represented the program's target labor force and audience, in that all of the later interviewees were involved in the local creative economy, from artists and creators to performers and academics. In all, I spoke over an hour each with more than forty residents who saw *Treme* as fans, critics, workers, or all of the above.[8]

Much of my initial discussions with others seemed to hinge on an investment in the city's authenticity: the special and unique character of New Orleans and, by extension, its people. From the airing of the pilot episode, *Treme* gave its viewers an opportunity to take a stand on what they love and hate about the mediatization of New Orleans. In general, viewers dismissed the media representations of the city as inauthentic at best. Another short-lived post-Katrina TV series, *K-Ville* (2007), drew mockery for its faux southern drawls and made-up cultural traditions, such as "gumbo parties." At worst, films set in New Orleans perpetuated damaging stereotypes, especially of an undifferentiated South. One interviewee elaborated this in a personal way:

> It's painful to me because New Orleans has a lot to offer [filmmakers], but we get passed over and typecast as a regional area. Sometimes we get lumped in with people from Texas or Alabama because the accents are indiscernible to a lot of people in the country. [. . .] It hurts when people from Hollywood come here and want to do sets of plantation homes and magnolias. (Technology worker, male, 29)

Following literary conceits, films set in New Orleans have historically stigmatized the place as an ugly or exotic twin of other American cities, thus representing the city as one end of the binary between "hedonism and piety, beauty and death, illusion and reality, and cosmopolitanism and provincialism."[9] According to interviewees, the tax-credit policy didn't necessarily assist in elevating better portrayals, more often erasing any sense of the local place, either behind green screens and generic sets or by redressing the city as somewhere else, such as Jackson, Memphis, or even the *Dawn of the Planet of the Apes* (2014). In contrast, *Treme* self-consciously sought to reflect the place, or at least hold a mirror to one of its reflections. In interviews and focus groups, speakers' first comments mimicked those that could be found in the local newspaper, which translated and praised the program's faithful archiving of local culture.

Nearly everyone compared *Treme* to this long roster of past films and programs based in New Orleans. Fans cited the authenticity of the smallest details, from the proper pronunciation of particular words in a neighborhood dialect, to the restaurant regular who is called to be in a scene filmed there.

> Like when [the Mardi Gras Indian chief character] Lambreaux holds out his finger and says "Feel that," because a real Indian has calluses from doing their own sewing.

It's just a very minor detail, but then the program apologizes when they don't do something that's not absolutely accurate.[10] (Lawyer, male, 58)

[I remember] the blue tarps and contractors blowing off the work [of rebuilding the city]. That detail stuck with me because I was working for a contractor then. (House-cleaner, female, 37)

The way they treat costumes [on *Treme*]. I mean I have a closet full of costumes and it's not just for Mardi Gras. It's just part of living here. (Barista, male, 47)

It's like New Orleans *Cliff Notes*. (Interior designer, female, 31)

[It's] like a little classroom every week. (Student, male, 22)

These details indexed an archive, a collection of concrete details that pointed to the local culture. Sometimes these facts were so arcane that viewers had to go to the newspaper, the HBO website, the Facebook page, or fan blogs for translation. One twenty-two-year-old described introducing the program to his parents, "who had no clue about the show," because he thought they could help him decipher the details. "I said, 'Oh my God Mom, you have to see this. You might know some of the people on it and some of the terminology better than I do.'" As a result, he watched the program with his family each week.

Treme showed that within a community, an archive is more than a collection. In every episode, musical performance, food traditions, parade cultures, and accurately accented vernacular sayings were categories for understanding home as a coherent physical place—one under the threat of disintegration. "The show felt like home because I went through those things," said one woman in her mid-forties who was simultaneously telling her Katrina story. Through the verisimilitude and the public circulation of those relatively minute or ordinary details, the *Treme* archive communicated the exceptionalism of the city and its people. Through it, Simon and the other *Treme* creators joined the ranks of the city's literary "vernacular kin," such as William Faulkner, who used "voices of its racialized and displaced citizens" to create a community based on "improvisational acts of affiliation, across difference, between persons dedicated to the local, the regional, and the vernacular."[11] With respect, if not reverence, viewers called cultural references they recognized in *Treme* "loving," "diligent," and "engaged," thereby calling attention to both the items and the program creators who stitched them into the fabric of the script.

Public screenings gave viewers the opportunity to perform their recognition of subtle, if not arcane, knowledge buried in a phrase, a guest talent, or a musical number. One bar that hosted the weekly broadcasts tried to broaden this community of "those in the know" by distributing episode guides, complete with synopses and character summaries. Yet the more instructive cues to the meanings embedded in the program came in vivo, when audience members publicly laughed, booed, or made pithy gestures. These particular screenings were made all the more authoritative by replicating the rules of a library; once the program started, all unrelated commentary to the archive was shushed in reverence to the contents. At these moments, silent at times with their sudden emotional eruptions, I felt suspended between my own personal study of the archive and the communal solidarity of entering the archival space together.

This tension between the personal and the public archiving of New Orleans culture in the show was especially salient in the context of the post-Katrina diaspora. Diasporas use archives as a way of rallying a sense of community, especially in the face of exile or even extinction. Archives make those communities visible, affirming their existence, legitimating shared knowledge, and helping imagine utopian futures.[12] For the members of the diaspora, archives provide a repository of things to hold on to if they have to leave the city, or if they are not present at the time of disaster. Yet archives also give people something to identify with and embrace when they come to the city. The influx of migrants to the city post-Katrina frequently looked to the television archive of the city in becoming part of the community. The solidarity forged by all of these diasporic New Orleanians defending the culture was "magical and amazing," according to one female at a coffee-shop conversation, because it showed "a sheer love of the city." Others hoped optimistically that, together, they would recover, restore, and renew the most endangered pieces of the culture. With little or no prompting, interviewees added their own stories to the archive they entered through the screen.

TREME AND ORDINARY TRAUMA

Another recurring feature in my research was when interviewees schooled me about New Orleans as a place. They would frequently start by telling me how New Orleans is, before telling me how *Treme* "gets it" right or wrong. For example, one interviewee, an older African-American gentleman, started to tell me, as many others would, "New Orleanians have their own authentic culture." He then said with a smirk, "Like when [the local actress] Phyllis Montana tells her husband [in a scene in *Treme*] that he came home that night 'smelling like cigarettes and pussy,' that was her line. Nobody outside of New Orleans could have thought of that anyway." At the moment, I think he was trying to catch me off my guard, but what really shocked me was how he could have divined that it was her line—that she had created it. Then I knew he was not kidding. A former mailman, this interviewee said he knew Montana because he used to deliver disaster-aid checks to her flood-ravaged neighborhood in New Orleans East.

By virtue of beginning the series and its storyline so soon after the disaster, *Treme* encouraged survivors to reflect similarly on the smallest details of their own post-Katrina stories.

> [In my FEMA trailer] my shower didn't work. My refrigerator didn't work. The heat was off in the middle of the winter. It was just irritating. We kept calling these people,

and we're dealing with the contractor, and we're screaming at each other because they said they're gonna show up and they didn't. There was all this constant frustration. Everyone was going through that. The first season [of *Treme*] was so good. When [the character] Ladonna cut into her roofer to do the work, I thought, yes, I've had those. I've had screaming battles with my contractor. It was a very intense time. (Landlord, female, mid-60s)

I could hardly help from being moved [by the show]. There were little nuances in there that I didn't even recognize. Some of the ways we talk. Some of the things we say and no one else says. And [the characters] said it in just such a way like we would. Like when the trombone player asks, "How's your mama?" He's not just saying that line. He's truly asking it. [. . .] Katrina put me in a place where I was willing to help people. We became a community like never before. (Barista, male, 47)

While these highly personal stories differed, they also spoke to viewers' own archival impulses, in making sense both of New Orleans as a place and of their own experiences there. Beyond the temporality of the program's broadcast, *Treme* seemed to elicit those impulses through conventions that resonated with residents' sense of home. Simply put, "The show was close to home," a viewer and tour guide told me. "There was a connection."

Even as loyal viewers scoured *Treme* for inconsistencies, factual errors, and lapses in creative license, they related to the details emotionally, if not therapeutically. The retelling of the past in terms of the present should come as no surprise. In classic psychoanalytic theory, the archive and therapy are codependent. The therapist records the patient's external utterances—vocal, corporeal—in an effort to later reread the archive as a window into an internal state. The archive is thus a technology for storing not just the evident past, but all of the traces that later can be reordered in some future story.[13] Many interviewees clearly wanted this reordering of the details, citing the city's people, including themselves, in their mental notebook. These stories were thus alternatives to the more epic and linear narratives of struggle, recovery, and rebirth. They tapped into a surplus of emotions—including sorrow, anger, and joy—that often exceeded the timescale of the program and its periodization of trauma. In some cases, viewers read the contemporary program through a thicket of historical details that sometimes carried back to the founding of the city. In other cases, not necessarily exclusive of the former ones, our conversations focused on current recovery efforts as the traumatic source.

With the exception of a few sporadic flashbacks, *Treme* was set in the period that locals still refer to as "post-K." In doing so, the program largely avoided representing the traumatic event. The montage of stills and clips in the opening credits combined a few iconic storm images in a scrapbook of other scenes drawn from daily life or ripped from the headlines. The absence of this weather specter was comforting to many viewers who were fatigued after numerous documentaries proceeded to repackage, even memorialize, disaster. Rather, they expressed relief that the program tackled the emotional weight of traumatic events that happened in the years following the event, including those referenced in the previous chapter. "The first two months were so intense, and I think the show shows that in a really accurate way, just how intense everything was," as one viewer explained.

The uncanniness of these fictionalized scenes based on reality and laid out in seemingly real time generated their own returns to interviewees' repressed emotions. One woman in her thirties, who watched with her friends, said the show was part of her own "grieving process" after the storm. She said she wanted to view the series with a group with whom she felt safe, because she still cried when an episode revived an old memory. The friend sitting by her side agreed, adding that his own tears were less forthcoming than they were in the past, but that the years since Katrina in *Treme* still felt like the present. In a similar way, another viewer thought *Treme*'s fictional world was "more healing . . . unguent" than documentaries, because it got her to laugh about her past. "You can't really joke about something you're hurting about," she explained. As if to repeat these returns, a few viewers mentioned the desire to watch the same episodes again in the search for more embedded nuances that they might ponder and cherish in the future. More commonly, interviewees expressed the desire to linger in the story itself. Fans talked how much they appreciated the slowed temporality and languid pacing in the program, especially in the first season. The long takes without rapid cross-cutting between scenes and characters evoked the sense of time stretched out. In these moments without much movement, the past seemed still like the present, the future foreshadowed but far away. Fans of the program countered critics of this languid pacing. "Things happened kind of slowly back then," recalled one viewer. Another compared the sensation of living in the city after Katrina to "Waiting for Godot," referencing a story in which the rescuer never arrives.

At its best, the combination of narrative elements and synchronic slowdowns in *Treme*'s fictional world evoked an emotional realism that imitated the conditions of perpetual crisis that have defined life for residents in New Orleans since Katrina. From episodic disasters to ongoing political and economic scandals, the era of what literary scholar Lauren Berlant calls "crisis ordinariness" infers that the media representation of crisis as a moment to be overcome has become normalized and diffused into everyday feelings of anxiety and unease. While most media still revel in portraying crises that victims face and surpass, any media representation of an impasse or a stalemate staves off the feeling, at the very least, of either resettling into normalcy or hurtling into the next crisis. For Berlant, media stories that feature stasis or avoid closure can be progressive alternatives to a reality so grim. Their spectators can find peace in the times when they can reflect without having to act.[14]

These temporal impasses were the subtexts in my focus groups when members debated the ongoing social problems that were not only threaded through the storylines in *Treme* but that also exceeded their diegetic timelines. Poor schools and the "charter-ization" of public education, the decline in services for the infirm and mentally ill, the absence of local grocery stores with fresh food options, and the ordinariness of everyday violence against citizens were common themes in these discussions. Many *Treme* interviewees agreed that Katrina had just accelerated the injuries caused by political corruption, economic inequality, and social injustice. In the words of one viewer and native resident, "New Orleans is cyclical. . . . Political leaders have wanted to keep the people hungry and uneducated, angry and malleable." In this sense, watching *Treme* was a time to reflect on the political impasse implied in the term *recovery*.

At the same time, *Treme* was part of the emotion economy that motivated viewers to act on the feelings that surfaced through the show. This is the cruel optimism that faith in the future can cure what ails the individual at present, according to Berlant. My interviews that followed a screening were always the most dramatic when viewers plotted themselves in *Treme*'s post-K timeline as the future defenders of the city. The host of the backyard screenings (quoted in this chapter's epigraph) suddenly took the floor after nearly an hour of quietly sitting while others talked. He said:

> I'm a fourth or fifth generation New Orleanian. This house and everybody here has a tie to this house. [Pointing at another man] He's like my phoenix. He talked me into rebuilding. The rebirth of this house is a lot of him inspiring me to do these things and really do a kind of monument to my family. Everything in this area was built by my great-grandparents. And I'm the last owner of the whole house here. I sat in this house after Katrina. I came back after a month. It was here. And it was dead quiet. Nothing's happening. *Treme* kind of reminds you of those times but also of the rebirth of the city and what it could be. (Contractor, male, 38)

While cueing his past and present memories, *Treme* also motivated him to envision a future for the city in which people could be preservationists or innovators, entrepreneurs or intermediaries, but each individual was responsible for defending the culture of the place. The projection of hope onto the urban hero was evident in public *Treme* screenings when the fictional characters directed their wit, charm, and anger to disarm anyone who was critical of the city in real life. I remember one screening during which the chef character Janine Desautel pitched a cocktail in the face of a restaurant critic playing a cameo. The critic in real life had written a scathing review of the city's food culture pre-Katrina, rhetorically asking "what exactly is it that we're trying to cherish and preserve" about New Orleans?[15] As if to answer him and anyone else who dissed the place, the crowded bar erupted in cheers and jeers for Desautel as their heroic proxy.

In its most overt call to help the city's recovery, *Treme* recruited residents to be part of its archival strategies by joining the production. Before the series even aired, many locals told me of their desire to be extras on this set but no others.

By the end of the first season's broadcast it was "the trend to work on the set, to be on the set, to be an extra, or have a friend that was an extra," said an African-American student who grew up in an affluent neighborhood Uptown. Said another devotee and would-be extra, "I would have to take off work and spend the day sitting around, but I would do it for *Treme*." These two statements encapsulated two sides of what would be *Treme*'s moral economy. On one hand, being an extra meant supporting the place through the program. On the other hand, extra-ing meant sacrificing time, and perhaps other earnings, in order to actually *do* very little, both somatically and symbolically.

In this regard, *Treme* was no different from other entities that directed the excess of emotions after Katrina toward a philanthrocapitalism based on corporate efforts, private volunteerism, and cheap or free labor. In the moment, the outsourcing of public disaster aid to private firms post-Katrina was already largely obscured behind empathetic and well-meaning volunteers who were channeled into the recovery.[16] Popular media, including *Treme,* were central to this ideological mission by making recovery into a personal duty. One newly arrived migrant to the city, a retired media professor, said he became an insider to the city's trauma by watching *Treme* weekly with a group of Katrina survivors:

> That experience certainly changed [my and my wife's] relationship to the show both in terms of the knowledge gained but also a sympathy towards it. People talked about how, you know, in the opening credits, there's the patterns of mold, and people said, "Yeah, that one looks like the one I have in my [flooded] house." And so you get connected to the show in ways that are very unusual. But *Treme* has been and continues to be this booster for New Orleans as a city. And right after Katrina that was critical. So I was a worshipper of *Treme* at that time because I felt people had given up on New Orleans, I mean really had given up. (Retiree, male, 61)

In the above passage, boosterism took on an almost spiritual devotion to the city as portrayed through the program. The spiritual alignment with *Treme* stemmed from an imagined belonging—first, to a community of empathy with the residents of a traumatized city; and second, to a television program imbued with the agency to help in the recovery. The production cultivated these feelings among viewers, and then exploited them.

PUTTING THE LOVE OF *TREME* TO WORK

The rhetoric of helping ordinary people in New Orleans was always part of *Treme*'s promotional strategy, from playing the role of the bard in the post-Katrina landscape to tithing local musicians and nonprofits that supported local culture. Among the virtuous acts that the production sponsored were charity balls for the corporate social venture Habitat for Humanity, where, for a $100 donation, one had the chance to see the cast in person as well as bid on local goods in a silent auction. The fine line between the celebration of ordinary culture and the cele-brification of the Hollywood-grade actors in the program was frequently crossed in these events in the name of social causes. Many of the program's stars became associated with local charity causes, from schoolbook and musical-instrument drives to home restorations in historically black neighborhoods.[17] By the time the shooting wrapped, Simon publicly claimed that *Treme* had tithed more than $500,000 to local charities.[18]

While celebrity philanthropy was certainly not unique to this television pro-gram,[19] the linking of each star's image to local and black culture followed the same recipe advocated in the city's own economic development plans for tourism. This odd confluence was especially evident during the 2013 Bicentennial celebra-tion of the Tremé neighborhood. Aside from the obvious mutuality between the place and the series, city planners referenced the show by sharing the same print font in order to promote the history of the "oldest Black neighborhood in the U.S." Banners showed the late Uncle Lionel, a brass-band player and personality of local musical culture, who also, as it happened, had played cameos on *Treme*. Lionel's ubiquitous image seemed to imply that the line between celebrating local culture in the public sphere and selling local culture in the private market was often in-distinguishable.

The contradictions that surrounded the profiteering from local culture and its preservation were most evident in the enrollment of Louisiana labor for the series. On one hand, producers knew that local hires accrued cost savings. Their payroll earned an extra 5 percent in tax credits. Local hires could save money on housing, transportation, even meals. On the other hand, the presence of so many locals in the program itself lent to producers' claims about the authenticity of the show. In particular, extras, also known as "background actors," did not need to do anything but hang around with others to give credence to the idea of New Orleans as a unique place—for example, a place where people congregate every day in their favorite bars and dark alcoves animated by old-timey jazz riffs and refrains. Merg-ing these two agendas, *Treme* producers framed local hires in terms of a moral economy. In it, the basis of the exchange relation between the company and the employee was founded in a social relationship that recognized the individual's unique role *in* the place and, thus, value *to* the place.[20]

The moral economy for *Treme* involved a series of ethically righteous and eco-nomically efficient trade-offs. In a phone conversation, the hiring director for the series explained to me that he learned that hiring residents was "the right thing to do" when he was a crew member on *The Wire*. Shot in his hometown of Balti-more, the director recalled feeling resentful when the production hired outsiders. In contrast, he said that *Treme* hired 220 crew from in state, compared to only 40 from out of state, in 2011. As stated in the previous chapter, an in-state hire does not necessarily mean that the person has been in the state for a long time. *Treme*, however, made a rare effort to collaborate with a community media nonprofit in sponsoring workforce training workshops. The workshops benefited both new and native New Orleanians, but the hiring director said that while the migrant hires brought more expertise to the project, the native hires brought added value in terms of their "natural knowledge" of the city. Local crew members streamlined the production schedule because "they know the Teamsters, and the bureaucrats, and also the residents. So they don't mind as much when you invade their neighborhood." Like soldiers in a battle to beat the budget, he said local hires helped "win the hearts and minds" of citizens about the program. Still, he added, his biggest challenge was to maintain continuity in the ranks. Nearly all of his skilled crew members left in 2010 to fill better-paying and higher-status gigs in major film projects. To avoid future turnover, the director said he began appealing to his weekly employees to develop a shared sense of loyalty in lieu of a fatter paycheck. "We're asking people to commit to us, and we will commit to them," he said. "People aren't in our production for the money. [. . .] You have to want to be here for what *Treme* is about."

In talking with the local residents who understood what *Treme* "is about," there was no doubt they thought the series participated in a moral economy that respected the place and its residents. Some said the production crews were especially courteous in notifying them about the closure of local streets. Others said they were unique in thanking residents with neighborhood parties, barbecues, and screenings. Local workers said they felt that fellow crew members treated them more respectfully than in other productions, such as by simply remembering their names or, in one case, helping an aspirant actor become part of the Screen Actors Guild. Although the wages for *Treme* did not deviate from union scales, workers mentioned that the production displayed other economic virtues, in what one punned was usually a "right-to-exploit state." Extras, in particular, said the program set a high bar by paying them $108 for a full day of work, and they were paid even if they were allowed to leave after a half-day. This figure, though tiny in relation to the size of production budgets, seemed meaningful to extras who were accustomed to as little as $80–100 for twelve to sixteen hours on set, with most of that time spent waiting around. In sum, the anecdotes told by local residents cast *Treme* as a different kind of film production from the others they had become familiar with in the city.

These ethical entreaties used in hiring local extras further defined New Orleans as a different kind of place from others that had a film economy. For one, the ethics of mutuality between producers and their employees substituted the usual "dues paying" mythology that saturates the Hollywood gig economy. In the myth, which was proffered historically by the trade press, temporary self-exploitation would eventually lead to a stable career in industry. In Southern California, this tale leverages a steady oversupply of cheap and willing labor.[21] *Treme* offered no

TREME: FILMING IN YOUR AREA

SET: PAYNE MEMORIAL CHURCH/ JAZZ FUNERAL   FILMING: TUESDAY, MARCH 31

Dear Residents and Business Owners,
"Treme," a television pilot for HBO, will be filming a JAZZ FUNERAL PROCESSION in your neighborhood on TUESDAY, MARCH 31 early afternoon –We will be POSTING NO PARKING in the 2200 – 2300 BLOCKS OF LOUISIANA and the 3300 – 2900 BLOCKS OF LASALLE, 2200 – 2300 BLOCKS OF TOLEDANO, THE 3300 - 1900 BLOCKS OF S. LIBERTY, 2200 – 2300 BLOCKS OF 7TH STREET, 2900 – 2800 BLOCKS OF LOYOLA, 2300 – 2100 BLOCKS OF 6TH STREE, 2100- 2200 BLOCKS OF WASHINGTON AVE. We thank all of our neighbors for their assistance in relocating their cars for the day as necessary. We are planning a thank you for the neighborhood and will keep you posted on the details. This will be our last visit to your neighborhood for the Pilot. Should we go to Series we look forward to working with you in the future. Thank you all for your great support. We have met wonderful people. Thank you for having us in your neighborhood.

Please let us know of any anticipated inconvenience so that we make work out a solution before it is a problem. We are working with the Mayor Office of Film and Video. Jennifer Day, the Director of the Office may be reached at 504-329-0665 to verify our credentials if we have not yet had the opportunity to meet you. We are also working with the New Orleans police to effect traffic control and monitor safety. During filming, we will be performing temporary traffic control and a Closure as before on Third Street and Daneel for safety. Please be aware however, particularly if you have young children and pets, of the increased activity in the

FIGURE 18. Flier distributed in a neighborhood for the *Treme* pilot. Residents noted the production crew's respectful tone in exchange for heavy use of their place.

such imaginary pathway. Instead, extras "worked" simply by being themselves. As one 2011 poster advertised:

> HBO's *Treme* needs "Festival-Goers"!
> Come and be a part of filming scenes to re-create a 2007 outdoor
>   Music Festival [. . .]
> WE NEED YOU!
> Let's show the world how New Orleans does it! [. . .]
> FREE Entry! FREE Festival Food! FREE Music![22]

Despite the call to have fun and enjoy free food and music, the plea "WE NEED YOU" also echoed the rhetoric of political recruitment. In the exchange, extras got more than a free show, they got the chance to convert their everyday lives into political capital. The producers made it clear not only that extras' ritual performance of the everyday was the source of their exchange value, but that showing everyday living in New Orleans on television was potentially a collective act of resistance to its erasure. By fusing the sense of the everyday as meaningless repetition with the sense of the everyday as a unique engagement with the world,[23] the production merged local cultural production and consumption for the series into a shared political project—as if watching the show, being on the show, and then promoting the show through one's social networks would help sustain other local circuits of music, art, or performance.

This call to do work was appealing to most extras, who told me that their labor was hardly laborious because they simply had to be themselves. Catching extra gigs during her off season was easy, according to a tour guide:

> One of the days I did extra work I was down on Frenchman street, which I go to all the time, and I went to the Spotted Cat [bar] and watched the Jazz Vipers [band], who are now the Cottonmouth Kings. Now [in season 2] a lot of my buddies have been on the show so chances are if I do it again, I'm going to hang out with them and get paid for it. (Female, 30)

Similarly, extras told me how they brought their friends, angled to see certain bands, or ate their fill of the decent smorgasbord, as if the job was more like a social event, if not a form of local tourism. Even the lead screen actress Montana said she did not feel her job was "like work [. . .] because I'm playing a character that's so much like myself."[24]

At some point, however, even regular extras realized how "extra boring" it was to repetitively be the kind of New Orleanian that producers wanted in the background.[25] In the age of reality programming, the directive to "be oneself, but more so" implicitly values stressing the parts of one's personality that fit the dramatic requisites of the program. In most cases, the result is that screen performers walk the line between representing themselves as unique individuals and reaffirming the stereotypes already associated with race, gender, and class.[26] On *Treme*, the extras needed to embody the features of its New Orleans archive, from ways of dressing and walking on screen to the postures and practices off screen. One interviewee, a schoolteacher and native New Orleanian, described these eager extras as a particular type she called "the super-New Orleanian." She explained, "They go to everything more than the people born here. They are the ones who know the musicians. They have all the connections. They are kind of in love with something they want to embrace much more than in the natural way [. . .] They can be almost arrogant about the *real* New Orleans." Even if exaggeratedly, these extras represented what it meant to be New Orleanians by becoming proxies for a place that they imagined was both outside of and part of themselves.

As a project that people saw as "more than just a film shoot," *Treme* articulated a complicated politics of belonging, to both its audiences and its potential workers. Fusing the sense of "being" and "longing,"[27] the series spoke to fans' yearnings to *belong* to a place—and to an identity in it—that felt stable despite the crises. To be an extra on the program allowed viewers to actualize their belonging to this partly real, partly fictional place. Extras spoke of a kind of doppelgänger effect, in which they already saw themselves living in the story.

> You're just looking around. It's like when I saw the big protest march in the last episode, I just keep seeing all these people from different parts of my life. They were all there. They were all extras so I joked that it was kinda like looking at a Sergeant

Pepper album cover, you know, to see all these people you recognize. (Nonprofit worker and singer, female, 47)

I kept expecting to see myself in the background because the scenes were so real to me. [. . .] I think there's some weird thing in my brain that I think I'm already a part of it. I think that would be really neat to be historically there and on film, to be part of New Orleans. (Composer, male, 47)

Both of these interviewees had moved to the city just a few years before Katrina. Now they wanted to not only "be in it because everyone else is in," as the first interviewee put it, but to be *remembered as being in it with everyone.* Whether represented by an album cover or a film, belonging expresses a reliance on its popular memorialization. Seeing their own lives unfold on the screen, these viewers wanted to be in the program, as if to merge the lived and its representation.

Treme offered the chance to memorialize the merger of self and image, to fix an attachment to the place even as its population moved and the city kept changing. This could be seen as a utopian project that allowed viewers to imagine alternate forms of belonging in modern life, a point that Elspeth Probyn makes in defining her own queer identity.[28] At the same time, *Treme* froze the dynamic movement of belonging and attachment through its own standard production practices. That is, once some fans signed on to be extras in the production, they no longer had equal footing with the community they projected on the screen. In this way, the film economy flattened the viewers' fantasies of belonging into a less satisfying exchange relation.

In illustrating how the program severed the utopian possibility between constructing the place and the desire to belong to it, I talked to extras about who was included and who was excluded from episodes based on real events. Two women, for example, decided to volunteer their vacation time for the 2011 season's reproduction of the 2007 Jazz Fest, as described in the call for extras above. For the women, Jazz Fest was an annual festival they had attended since its beginnings and when they began annual pilgrimages from their hometowns of New York and San Francisco. Although they were gainfully employed female professionals and had never before been extras, they said they wanted to belong to the community that they felt *Treme* shared with them. They woke up at 6 A.M. that morning, prepared their bags, and trudged down to the city fairgrounds on an unseasonably cold day. They spent the entire day there, a gift of themselves that they felt was hardly reciprocated by the crew. Instead, said one of the two, "What they did was the ever-present, self-referential, congratulatory New Orleans shit. You know which you just never hear the end of." More interesting to them was who was in the crowd.

Female 1: It was a very interesting mix of people in there.

Female 2: Just like New Orleans. Only more black people attended that [*Treme*] festival [set] in 2007 than you would ever dream [did in real life].

F1: Right. There were a lot of black people. They brought in schools. They brought in a couple of schools.

F2: You know there're no black people at Jazz Fest. It's too expensive.

VM: Yeah.

F2: [. . .] New Orleans is extremely integrated in flocks. I understand, you know, the thing about having to make that scene. But the reality is not really that. So I thought this was going to be a version of that today too [at the Jazz Fest shoot].

VM: And yeah that was interesting. I mean . . .

F2: I said to [my friend], "Now listen. They're probably going to make us leave, so just be prepared to be rejected you know the minute we arrived." But it was no problem.

F1: They took everybody who showed there.
[. . .]

F1: What I saw was that people were just excited. The combination of Jazz Fest and *Treme* [. . .] It is very, very ideological almost.

F2: Also another thing that would never, in a million years, happened at Jazz Fest. This black boy's school, pretty little boys, ages ten, eleven, twelve. They did [. . .]

F1: Mosh pit. They did a mosh pit.

F2: In the Blues Tent. And they did this incredible dancing, this line dancing. They were wonderful, but then they just started jumping. You know that would be dispersed immediately if you ever even saw that many black people or young people at the Jazz Fest.

VM: So was that part of the narrative?

F2: No.

VM: That was spontaneous?

F1: There wasn't even a camera on site. They had a lot of school buses, had a lot of kids come. They had this tiny little bunch of kids in uniform. They were so cute and Big Sam [the musician on stage] did the Hokey Pokey with them [off stage].

F2: I had pictures.

In this passage, the women illuminated a politics of belonging to the place evoked in *Treme,* one that seemed to overemphasize the racial diversity of its members, but that nevertheless excluded the young, black boys in the production. While the women expected to be turned away initially from the shoot as cultural outsiders, they felt like they succeeded instead in witnessing the most authentic performance of the day.

It was in these moments of asserting their belonging to New Orleans but not to its representation that many extras felt unmoored in describing the gap between *Treme*'s version of "home" and their own social lives, what Probyn terms television's *unheimlich* home.[29] In other words, collecting Facebook likes and cheers of recognition at a bar screening may have consolidated the meaningfulness of appearing on the show with the importance of rebuilding the city. Yet, to quote an essay likening New Orleans to one of Italo Calvino's *Invisible Cities,* the television show could not reconcile images of a city that "was more difficult to explain to the tourists" but nonetheless had given them a "postcard" of its everyday.[30] Another disappointed attendee at that particular Jazz Fest shoot said she had felt tricked into working for free and left the fairgrounds early, as if a spell had been broken from a curious disease: "It was Jazz Fest fever. You're in Jazz Fest and [the *Treme* signs] say come back tomorrow for more music so I went. It was a trap."

It was this sense of the *unheimlich,* or the uncanny, that seemed to unravel both these workers and viewers enamored with the healing powers of *Treme* over the place they called home. The uncanny speaks to experience of strangeness in modern life, reminding us that, even at home, social forces operate to pull us apart. For the medical philosopher Andrew Edgar, the uncanny is a natural feature of human life, but one that is typically repressed under experiences that we deem more "authentic" or "everyday."[31] Although the *Treme* archive celebrated the everyday and authentic, its production around town ironically leveled these elements into objects that seemed strange, inauthentic, and unlike home. Herein Edgar poses the political potential of the uncanny, not just to reveal the myth of an "authentic" culture, but also to reveal the political and economic structures that alienate people from their sense of place.

NAVIGATING UNEASY FEELINGS IN THE PRODUCTION OF THE BIG EASY

Over the years that *Treme* was shooting on location in New Orleans, the series became wrapped up in the daily lives of people who came into contact with the program through experiences that could seem commonplace. The wide geographic scope of the project, the enlistment of local employees, and the voluminous integrations of the signs of the place all contributed to this uncanny merger of culture and film economy—not least for those already working in the city's creative sectors. For them, the extremely personal address of the show, in a place where they felt at home, felt distinctly *unheimlich*:

> [My boyfriend] was driving around town and I looked over and I saw along Saint Claude [Avenue] that there were a couple of [Mardi Gras] floats. And this was the middle of summer. And I'm like, "What are these floats doing here?" I thought it was a prank and somebody stole them. And then I saw they had the same themes as the

floats from that year [after Katrina]. And then I'm like, "What the hell is going on?" Because they reused this float. And then we found out later that they had recreated Mardi Gras because [the *Treme* crew] was looking for extras for that scene. I was like, "Oh *now* it makes sense." I see more and more of that all the time. (Recycling coordinator, female, 46)

You know what it is? It's like a map of your life. Like [. . .] Oh, this clearly shows that other people value the set of downtown experiences that I value because they're going to the same place. They're filming at [places like] BJs and the Hi Ho and Saturn Bar and Satsuma and, like, they're building a world out of the places I live in. So it's like a fictionalized map of my time in New Orleans. (Teacher, female, mid-40s)

While many residents of Los Angeles no doubt experience the uncanny in their daily encounters with film productions, New Orleans residents spoke of a particularly fraught return of the repressed. *Treme* provided a jolt to viewers' sense of self in a place that was so available to being represented, rescripted, and revisioned, and that, at exactly the same time, the film economy participated in that transformation. For all of the creators' embedded commentaries on local politics and culture, the ghostly presence of the film industry itself created quite a bit of reflection on what could not be part of the archive because it was unspeakable.

"There is like stuff you go out and see and experience every day of the week and all of a sudden, it's on tape forever," said a middle-aged man in a group setting. "Like it's the really cool stuff you can't . . . articulate, but it's right there and you can enjoy it whenever you want." He postulated that the program helped those still exiled from the city maintain a connection with a place they loved. By imagining these viewers as those who were displaced, viewers in the city could see the program as supplanting a sense of place that was still relevant to the city without being the whole city. After all, the speaker spoke of going to the places that *Treme* references. Another male sitting next to him agreed, saying that the show was a testament to preserving people's memories of a place that has already been lost to "condos and these yogurt places around." Although he was referring to urban renewal and gentrification in any number of other American cities, these trends, also present in New Orleans, could speak to the displacement that anyone in the city might feel from the place memorialized by the television program. In one of the focus groups at my house, a friend of mine explained how watching *Treme* reminded her of a place she could no longer experience even though she lived in the city. She had a new baby and a full-time job, but she recognized the local culture she loved on the television program. She said, "Some of these things [on *Treme*] show that even if we don't use the culture—and I can be uptight, and work too much, and I cannot go out late just any night—but just knowing the people in the next block live like that makes me happy here." The contrast between her *life,* which could be anywhere, and that *place,* where people live as in *Treme* implied an unusual affection for a culture that surrounds the place but not all its residents.

In this way, the archival qualities of the show were animated, but also outside of everyday life, for people whose social conditions seemed to prevent crossing into that other world.

My conversations often revealed the thin line between personal memories of the city and *Treme's* memorialization of New Orleans as a place that blurred the line between what was familiar and what was strange. The feeling of the former could be tucked away, a comforting reminder that this was one's home. In talking about what made New Orleans a place, interviewees repeatedly stressed both the ephemerality and the routineness of unique, everyday encounters in a unique public culture that celebrates difference, diversity, and tolerance—what has been characterized as "creole urbanism" that makes the city exceptional in relation to the rest of the United States.[32] While some speakers harked back to some origin stories about the city's exceptionalism, what became evident in all cases is that they saw themselves the constituents of the exception. The flip side of their understandings of this place as intimate, unique, and authentic was their assumptions about social relations in the city in terms of race, gender, and class. Comments about race relations, for example, could easily manifest what the literary critic Santiago Colás calls the "creole symptom" in that they express desire for a utopian creole identity without acknowledging the colonial relations that produced it.[33]

In viewer interviews, the creole symptom was expressed as a fantasy of cultural interconnectedness. One of the most popular games around *Treme* screenings was the retelling of who knows who, what, and where in a way that showed the intimacies with the New Orleans diaspora. Through these games, I learned that the real person that a character was based on in the program was the roommate of my friend's baby daddy. I found out that he had tried to seduce my friend, but he also taught her daughter music at her charter school. On further inquiry, I then knew his sister, who works for the same institution as I, and that he later dated someone else whom everyone apparently knew. Similar games connected me with the chiefs and the chefs, the creatives and all of the other character roles on *Treme*. This was one sense of community integration. It marked a particular milieu in the city of musicians and teachers, lovers and parents. It was intergenerational, polyamorous, and even multiracial within this shared habitus. As one viewer had remarked to me, "New Orleans is extremely integrated in flocks."

At the same time, viewers' desire for the creole could not be believably sustained in the program. Many interviewees commented on the lack of well-rounded characters hailing from the city's black middle class, or from its gay and lesbian communities, as a major oversight in understanding the mixing of different social groups across racial and class lines. In group screenings, audience members rejected the ways in which the program dissolved the degrees of separation between social groups through the trope of intermarriage. In these instances—for example, uniting a Dutch musician with the daughter of a Vietnamese fisherman; an ambitious

Asian-American musician with a lazy, white "trustafarian"; and a creole dentist with an African-American bar owner—the dream of creolization was simply too far-fetched to be believed. Residents felt that these integrations were neither familiar nor a fantasy that could be imagined in the real New Orleans. These were people, in other words, who did not share the same place. For them, *Treme*'s New Orleans was different from the one the viewers felt at home with.

Most people simply expressed these aspects of the show as strange or unreal, setting up a dichotomy between what was real and what was authentic. For these same people agreed that *Treme* was authentic, more so than any other portrayal of the city. Yet the ways in which the show animated these authentic details could still not match reality. For example, an African-American business owner, artist, and native resident of the city explained to me his take on an episode the night before.

> You know, [*Treme*'s creators] have the D.J. Davis talking [on the radio] to Manny Fresh, who's a local rapper. [Fresh] was a part of Cash Money [Records] and the Hot Boys [rappers] and stuff like that. But the way Davis was talking to him seemed to me a little condescending to me. And Manny was dissing him a bit. *I think if that exchange went on in reality it wouldn't have gone anywhere like how they portrayed it.* Manny would be like, "Hey fuck you. Don't even waste my fucking time on the phone." And that would have been the end of it.
>
> Because, you know, I'm like from a poor neighborhood in New Orleans. The one thing that can get you is that people have to think you're being sincere, especially when you're doing the racial dynamics. So if there's even a small hint you might be kind of phony, if you know what I mean, then forget about it. It ain't going to happen. And in that little exchange on *Treme,* the dude just seemed phony as hell. [emphasis added]

Although this particular viewer said that *Treme* was the closest that any media program had come to resonating with local viewers, it fell short in capturing what he called the "layers" of cultural exchange in the city. Drawing on his own organic knowledge of communication scripts across racial and class lines, his example highlighted one such exchange between a real rap star, who rose to celebrity from a poor black neighborhood, and a *Treme* character, a white hipster from an affluent background. The cameo appearance in the program perhaps made it even more important for the fictional character, based on a real local elite and recreated by a celebrity outsider, to *recognize* the rapper's race and class status. In a similar critique, this viewer rejected a scene in the same episode in which local policemen beat a black musician in public for bumping into a squad car. "I'm not saying that would never happen, but it's the exception," he said, adding that such police brutality would be more likely to happen across class lines, such as when "you have all these new people coming in and calling in to complain everyday" about street musicians in front of their private property. Inadvertently, interviewees such as this one implicated the new gentrifiers that *Treme* attracted to the city as the ones who would transform race relations in the city.

These somewhat oblique critiques of the film economy recurred in the interviews as the uncanny feelings stimulated by a particular scene. Another middle-class woman talked about a bar scene in which the pole dancers were dancing silently in the background, but the bartender in the foreground had an eloquent recitation on the state of crime in the city. She wondered why the male bartenders and service workers got to be bards for the city, while the women were voiceless props. She summarized, "There's a whole segment of the popular, the people, or maybe several segments missing." As it turned out, her daughter was a dancer, occupying one of the most lucrative jobs in post-Katrina New Orleans.

Meanwhile, those viewers who worked for the love of program had their own strange encounters. One recurring extra on the set, a white woman in her fifties, said the crew was one of the "nicest" she had ever met. Even so, she was excluded from every shoot that was supposed to be in "a black part" of town. "I found out they are a bit choosy how they put people together," she said. "They just pointed at all the black people and say we want you and everyone else can go home." While this wasn't a problem, she said, there was at least one time she felt slighted when producers came to a free, weekly screening of the show in her neighborhood. The episode replayed an emotive scene she recalled in her own life before the producers combed the audience to be extras in another scene drawn from real events. "I said I was there the night [the musician] Glen David Andrews was arrested.[34] [The producers] didn't really believe it too much, you know. They thought that was kinda strange, but [one of the mothers of the band members] came out and said she was glad I was there. That meant more to me than the money." Here the feeling of estrangement from the production itself was recouped by another member of the crowd who was a Tremé resident and a *Treme* viewer.

In writing about the uncanny as a natural feature of modern life, Edgar also sees it as a political phenomenon. While the feelings of displacement or that things are out of place may seem existentially wrong, even something that has to be recuperated or made whole again, the person feeling the uncanny may react both by internalizing their feelings—as in the case of the extra who endures being cut from the scene—and externalizing their feelings by telling others.[35] The uncanny reactions that viewers had to *Treme* unraveled a mythical creole urbanism, belied the creole symptom, and gave texture to real events that the film economy had flattened in the process of representing them. This potential seemed to me to be the most radical affront to the film economy that *Treme* could muster.

Perhaps unsurprisingly, then, the most eloquent critique of *Treme* came from someone who worked with the industry, whose sense of place and displacement were conjoined with the success of a local film economy. I was complaining to her that the series felt the need to have a Mardi Gras episode each season.[36] That

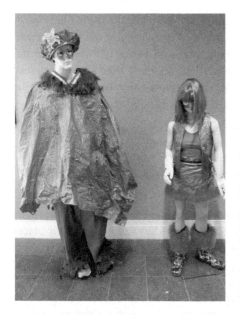

FIGURE 19. An example of *Treme*'s detailed archive of the city's history and culture. Here, the blue tarps of traumatic Katrina memories are repurposed as carnival suits for an episode portraying Mardi Gras 2006, which were then displayed in a local art museum as a tourist attraction. From "Well Suited: The Costumes of Alonzo Wilson for HBO's *Treme*," The Ogden Museum of Southern Art, January 24 to March 31, 2013. Photo by Vicki Mayer.

may be, she responded, but *Treme* could never capture the temporal feeling of everyday life:

> [T]he manic intensity of the place: the fresh donut sign, and the politician is there having lunch . . . and Ken is playing the tuba in the neutral ground with a dancing baby in front of him . . . and then one of the stand-still silver guys comes riding a bike down the street. Like all of the craziness that just happens constantly because of the construction of the city. I don't think that sense of the daily insanity comes through, and [*Treme*] I guess reifies the traditional concepts through Mardi Gras, which is that we party a lot.

Treme created a place that reified lived experiences by making them into static goods for sale. This was a critique that came up in numerous conversations, often punctuated with the word *corny* to detect words that are opposite of culture. People also used terms like *commodity, product,* and *cartoonish*—words that point to what happens when authenticity is a mode of marketing places. The distillation of time in exchange for a rapid travel through space spoke to an economics of *Treme*'s archive, in which everything (and space) was flattened to have the same value. But "that moment of magic isn't sellable in the same way."

In these ways, the critiques of *Treme* grounded a popular distancing from the local tourism economy, while also realizing how the film economy hailed them to be tourists in their own place. Despite the careful collecting of details in the show, the whole was actually less than its parts, showing "all the bling and flash of New

Orleans [without] any real depth," said one artist who hated the show. Many viewers felt that the program played its own role in gentrifying and selling the spaces
discussed in chapter 2, especially those associated with a sense of folksy authenticity.[37] Another resident who did not watch *Treme* regularly lived in its namesake
neighborhood and witnessed its transformation into a cultural tourism hub. She
defended the show as a form of consciousness-raising publicity for outsiders:

> Even if it's not bringing any dollars into the economy, it's a good thing to show our
> neighborhood [...] So when people come to the neighborhood, they get a little sense
> of it. They go to a bar and experience something. They feel good. Maybe they ask new
> questions because they're surrounded by something foreign. (Community outreach
> organizer, female, 35)

Like a music-festival promoter or an ecotourism guide, *Treme* used the allure of its
foreignness and entertainment value to educate outsiders about the specific places
worthy of their dollars rather than the city's economy as a whole. The TV show
gave visible evidence of which people, practices, and places mattered most for the
city's public–private redevelopment.

As those dive bars, clubs, and corner stores came to stand for New Orleans in
heritage tourist circles, some viewers recognized—often with a reflexive sense of
hypocrisy—how they also went there. In fact, their unique place was *not* exceptional at all. For an ultra-reflexive friend of mine, this political recognition was a
process:

> A bunch of my friends actually just came back from Puerto Rico and I realized the
> tone of the white traveler in them. The [sense of] "I've discovered something" and "I
> went to these places" and these are the very specific places. You know, I would never
> go on a cruise. I would never go to the Hard Rock Cafe. I would only go to these
> places that I deemed to be authentic. And they're authentic because they belong to
> brown people, and they have very specific names to them, and I know them now. I
> know that that was me too. Like when I moved to Mexico, I felt a possessiveness over
> Mexico that only the white traveler can have. And it's similar to that. David Simon
> and I, viewer of *Treme*, we can identify these places as real places. And I can therefore
> understand them and also feel like I have a glimpse into another world that's different
> and distinct from me because I know these things. And I mean, God, I have a bunch
> of ambivalence too. Your neighborhood has changed. Our neighborhood is actively
> going through that change right now. (Teacher, female, mid-40s)

Even as interviewees frequently bemoaned how *Treme* told all their cultural secrets, they could also recognize their own complicity in making places into their
secrets and trading them as insider knowledge about others. All the while, interviewees were aware that at the end of the night, home was somewhere else. If
these critiques of the structural forces that construct and then reify the creole were
latent in my conversations with others, they were always just below the surface.

Conversations about these contradictions were in some ways the most difficult I had with viewers, particularly my friends and acquaintances. They involved the recognition that *Treme* hailed a diaspora that no doubt filled the requisites of a niche audience. Educated and overwhelmingly white in my own sample, these viewers were able to either afford the premium channel subscription or they easily entered the social venues where the program was free, but the drinks and the discussions were bound to the social milieu. They knew this. I knew this. The show ultimately generated an excess of emotions around this fact that could not be contained by it and, luckily, would not be. The series ended, but the conversations have continued.

TREME AS HOLLYWOOD SOUTH'S ALIBI AND INSTRUMENT

Treme's production was self-referential in commenting on Hollywood South's role in the city's future. From the beginning, Simon challenged the industry to show a national audience how New Orleans culture was "about something much bigger [. . .] in the context of all the political [news] and all the problems and all of the distopic things that have happened post-Katrina—if you can't [make] a story out of that, shame on you."[38] The LLC hired workers who insisted it was different from all the other productions because it left people "with a better feeling for New Orleans," in the words of a creative director. *Treme* gave visible evidence of Hollywood's power to shape a city through its representation.

For four years, *Treme* advertised culture under an urban policy that needed more consumers. It expanded viewers' vocabularies to include second lines and Mardi Gras Indians, while seeing the damaging harm caused by police profiling and market exclusion. In an era in which neighborhoods needed to prove their economic value for reinvestment, the program broadened the map for film locations by purposely seeking areas of the city no one had filmed in before.[39] It gave everyone the rationale to support New Orleans's recovery through cultural consumption. Like the tourism industry, the series defined positive urban development in aesthetic and emotional terms. No other media production before or since *Treme* has so thoroughly illustrated such synergies with the aims of the city's post-Katrina development strategies.

The politics of representation, however, had its limits. One question that stumped everyone in my many years of discussing *Treme*'s realism was why the series never represented its own industry's presence in the creative economy. This absence was most glaring to me in an episode that dwells on the scandalous use of details to distract police from their duties, with nary a mention that Hollywood South is the biggest detail buyer, as relayed in chapter 2. The omission, while

FIGURE 20. Local synergies in selling the city back to itself via the series *Treme*. Photo by Vicki Mayer.

perhaps understandable as an oversight, reinforced how *Treme*'s archive of cultural contexts was incomplete. In fact, the series referenced the film industry only once in its four-year run. That instance was in a victim-to-victor vignette about Tia Lessin, a "self-described street hustler" whose amateur video footage of the hurricane and its aftermath resulted in a Hollywood red-carpet premiere.[40] For all its realism, *Treme* chose to tout and not trounce Hollywood's most cherished myth of meritocracy.

It was a faith in the merits of a local film economy that perhaps brought the cruelest optimism to those who believed that the show's success portended their own futures and fortunes. In the words of a twenty-something New Orleanian looking for stable work in the creative sector: "I guess we want the show to justify us being here, you know. People ask us [why we are here after Katrina] and we can say, 'the arts' and all. We certainly know the drawbacks of being here too. If the show is doing well, we all feel like we are doing well." This cathartic case, however, hurts more than heals. Optimism in the face of a film economy politically designed to allow the monopoly of public resources depends on a race to the bottom "driving down pay rates, benefits, and job satisfaction for media workers around the world."[41]

Hope for this creative economy based on supply-side subsidies has done little to relieve the everyday precariousness of its workforce. In one poignant example of this from my research, one of the local cultural-heritage celebrities featured in an episode of *Treme* never saw her own cameo, because she could afford neither to pay HBO nor to fix her car on the day she was to watch it at my house. From the vaunted musician to the supporting service worker, the local creative labor force has served the concentration of private wealth with its flexibility to move from "security to insecurity, certainty to uncertainty, salary to wage, firm to project, and profession to precarity"—all these workers performing "with smiles on their faces."[42] *Treme* may have got "it right" in lionizing cultural workers and highlighting their struggles, but it could never "make it right" for them by being the poster child for creative boosterism, philanthropic charity, labor volunteerism, and the redistribution of a small portion of its public dividends back to a few select artists. These efforts may have made citizens feel good about the potential of Hollywood South, but they did little to reveal (if they didn't actively obscure) the Faustian bargain New Orleans made with the film economy.

(Almost a) Conclusion

Facing a shortfall of up to $2 billion, the Louisiana legislature began in 2015 to seriously reevaluate the policy that had engineered Hollywood South. The state had approved over $220 million in film tax credits in the previous year. Meanwhile, the state's higher-education and health-care systems stood to declare bankruptcy in the face of massive cuts. For the first time, a key economic adviser stated, "we are in a situation today, with the size of this [film funding] program relative to the challenges you are facing with the state budget, that it is now in direct competition with some other state priorities."[1] In addition to the sense that film now competed directly with other key spending priorities, critics came to the table armed with the state's own economic development study, which estimated the film program's cost at four times the revenue it generated, as well as a list of recent fraud cases that suggested the program had become a leaky corporate-entitlement scheme. For perhaps the first time since the passage of the 2002 incentive program, there was a flurry of public discussion in popular media.[2]

Driving home from work, I pulled over to listen to the afternoon disc jockeys on B97 (an Entercom FM pop station) "debate" film policy in late April 2015. Suddenly, the conversation that I heard so often among friends and acquaintances around Hollywood South was now in the public sphere. Beginning with the high costs of the policy to the state budget, the disc jockeys quickly cut to the chase:

> *Stevie*: But I can also see the counterargument.
>
> *T-pot*: Which is?
>
> *Stevie*: We get to see celebrities on the street. How cool is that?!

> *T-pot*: Yeah when else will we get to see [stars] Brad Pitt and Matthew Mc-
> Conaughey and [football star] Drew Brees together on a balcony in
> the French Quarter?

Weighing costs and benefits, the disc jockeys concluded that the aura of Hollywood has been well worth the price of productions. Down the street, they reasoned, New Orleans could be made up to look like Wall Street or anywhere else. People were earning good money making films. More people came and, ergo, more money rolled in.

> *Stevie*: Of course the argument is pretty strong that we could use the money
> those tax credits bring. If the tax credits go, that money goes away.
>
> *T-pot*: Yeah.
>
> *Stevie*: And of course we could use the money. But I'm not convinced we'd
> use the money right. [. . .] So if we could start using the tax money
> for other than, oh I don't know, *corruption* [. . .] then maybe we could
> consider it. But for now, how about you let the tax credits stay so we
> can have the coolness of having Brad Pitt walk down the street?
>
> *T-pot*: I don't know if that's a good trade-off but whatevs.
>
> *Stevie*: Either it's in the corrupt people's pockets or in Hollywood's pockets.
> And they're like here shooting movies.[3]

In balancing the emotional perks and the rational calculus, national recognition and local jobs, the disc jockeys finally rested their decision on their faith in the film economy over those elected to manage it. Ironically, state representatives across the country would be making the same arguments that the disc jockeys did in the months just preceding and proceeding from this staged debate.

After two decades of competition to be the low-cost leader for location shooting, Louisiana became one of a handful of states to suddenly question the script that film-industry lobbyists and their local boosters had authored together since the silent era. Yet the battle lines in the public sphere during 2015 were drawn between two elite factions of crony capitalists, leaving the aura of Hollywood South and its underlying financial logic relatively unscathed. With both sides leveraging local land and labor as both their alibi and their prize, the crisis in Louisiana, especially in light of many regions facing the same dilemmas, should be instructive in preparing for future battles between voodoo economics practiced by all monsters of the public till and creating a more local variation of "hoodoo economics" for the home team.

THE KING OF THE ZOMBIES VERSUS VAMPIRES

To understand the sudden about-face on the film tax incentive policy after such a long and dedicated romance requires a screenplay. The backstory dates to the era when Hollywood dominated locations and labor. Recalling the movie *King of the Zombies* (as presented in the Introduction), the current conjuncture might be called a sequel with vampires added. In it, the multinational Koch Industries has conjured a band of neoliberal vampires that try to suck the blood from all public investments in a common good. Led principally by the libertarian lobby Americans for Prosperity (AFP), together with other neoconservative groups, including the Tea Party and the Heritage Foundation, the vampires have fought for the repeal of any dedicated state funding for all creative industries, but especially for film and entertainment. In the true fashion of a cult horror flick, the new drama has featured a death match between these two dark forces.

In the months leading to the climactic clash, Louisiana Film Entertainment Association (LFEA) had been mobilizing to "speak with one voice regarding the positive economic impact the entertainment industry provides to Louisiana." Using social media and website advocacy campaigns to collect personal stories of the positive impacts of the film industry on individuals, the trade association adopted a grassroots-style populist defense of the policy, which, budget experts had charged, enriched very few at the expense of all Louisiana taxpayers.[4] To counter the wonks, in September 2014, LFEA's "Two Bucks Campaign" raised over $45,000 on the Kickstarter crowdfunding platform for a "landmark economic study" that would prove the value of the industry to government representatives.[5] Campaign supporters could post their uplifting stories on a Facebook site. Those people included several background actors (aka extras), a cupcake baker who caters, a television reporter who covers Hollywood South, a number of hotel and restaurant workers, and a bevy of film and communications college students. By January 2015, LFEA's efforts were in full swing. They organized their supporters to write personal letters to state House and Senate members, and then to don red t-shirts at the Capitol in protest of any policy changes that would eliminate their jobs or their lifelong dreams. At least some of those dreams involved winning the Kickstarter campaign itself, according to a script supervisor who donated $10,002 in return for LFEA producing her short film. "It baffles me whether anyone could wonder whether the tax incentives bring money into our state, because I see it every day," said the lucky winner to a local news crew.[6]

Given the budgetary shortfall, most lawmakers were convinced they had to at least appear to fix the program's most egregious violations of public trust. Under the banner of "mending without ending," the most conciliatory legislators proposed closing loopholes for auditor fraud, banning credit brokers with felony records, and prohibiting investors from taking their insurance premiums and airfare from the state till. The most vocal LFEA hero, Democratic State Senator Jean-Paul Morrell of New Orleans, balked at limiting incentives overall, preferring to target cuts to actors and producers making more than $3 million per production. He suggested a symbolic cap of certifying $300 million in film projects per year, a figure well above the current high watermark, and actually expanding credits to capture more locally generated and independent productions. "The film and movie production industry made possible by these credits has brought a new sense of innovation to Louisiana," Morrell argued. "The problems that have arisen are correctable and I will do everything in my power to ensure the future viability of this valuable program."[7]

Morrell's critics were unmoved. Likening the state tithes to "a 40-year-old son who won't get out of the house," one state representative authored a bill to cap the amount the state would reimburse tax credit buyers in a given year.[8] His metaphor of a deadbeat dependent was thematically consonant with the AFP's coordinated attacks, in 2014 and 2015, on regional film-industry incentives in North Carolina, New Jersey, Michigan, and Florida as "handouts" and "corporate welfare." The lineup of socially conservative Republicans behind the cap in Louisiana also fit the AFP's national efforts to blame Hollywood stars, for both their financial and their moral support of U.S. President Barack Obama's policy positions, including the 2010 Affordable Care Act (aka Obamacare), and challenges to "religious freedom" laws aimed at discriminating against LGBT citizens.[9] With both sides pitting creative enterprise against good governance and the inherent value of a private workforce over public regulations to protect workers, the King of the Zombies and the vampires waged war, each on the basis that only their side protects local workers.

With political clout and riches on par with Hollywood, the Kochs' campaigners took credit for killing film-industry tax incentives in North Carolina in 2014, along with Florida and Michigan in 2015; but Louisiana opted for another outcome.[10] The governor signed House Bill 829 into state law ninety minutes before the end of the 2015 session. Accepted by margins of eight to one in the House and two to one in the Senate, the bill severed the seeming elite ideological consensus for Hollywood South. Through the anger and tears, no one claimed the measure was a win for their side.[11]

The final law neither fed nor starved the film tax-credit program in any clear or unilateral way. It followed the admonishments of local labor defenders by increasing the residency period to be considered a Louisiana worker and lowering the minimum budget to allow indie filmmakers to earn film tax credits. It even added another 15 percent credit for screenplays optioned from Louisiana authors and recordings sampled from Louisiana musicians. The new expansions, for example, meant the state could offset up to 60 percent of a film budget that used a Louisiana resident's screenplay or music. From this, one might argue that Hollywood South would finally get an organic advantage by seeding the cluster of workers in its backyard.

At the same time, the law temporarily capped the ability of the state to pay the debts it had incurred in previous years, reserving $180 million per year until 2018. While the reimbursement cap was set at the amount the state had certified in 2011, the rule meant that productions that were certified as finished would be in line to see if the expenditures could be recouped in a given year. Although the productions hand off their tax credits to others through their brokers, the move likely would reduce the credits' overall market value in the coming years, so the move elicited howls from LFEA supporters and fiscal hawks alike.[12] In the deus ex machina to the budget drama, lawmakers decided to continue the romance of the film industry while draining some of its lifeblood, namely the guarantee of free money. Amid the uncertainty, the number of major Hollywood productions that were shot in the state plummeted in 2016.[13]

What the 2015 budget showdown in Louisiana ultimately demonstrated was the resiliency of Hollywood South as an ideal, despite its Gothic impacts on state coffers. While the King of the Zombies was wounded, the overall regime remained strong. Production companies turned, on a dime, to "Y'allywood" in Georgia and back to California, where legislatures in both states increased their subsidies to wear the mantle of film capital.[14] After two failed bids to repeal the cap, LFEA has held out hope that the political climate will change; because if the cap is repealed, then the policy in place actually *increases* the total state spending on filming. If not, Louisiana will likely face a backlog of over $200 million in unredeemed credits by 2019. Meanwhile, the vampires also won, continuing their assault on health and human services, public education, housing, and transportation, not to mention the arts and cultural programs that the film economy was supposed to uplift. They continued to deliver public lands and goods to the cold embrace of a privatized market. The national safety nets and protections all workers depend on have been so eviscerated by these undead overlords in recent years that the people living in states deciding whether to expand or repeal their film incentives have a limited horizon of alternative possibilities. In the process, new, expedient definitions of the "local" have changed what it means to live and work in New Orleans.

THE LACUNAE OF THE LOCAL IN LITTLE HOLLYWOODS

Through the various iterations of film and entertainment incentive policies, New Orleans's self-image as a unique and exceptional place has adopted new codes for understanding the worth of local culture and labor. In the lingo of the policy, "local" denotes simply a physical position, based on residency alone. Thus, the gaffer who arrives for six months supplies the same financial boon to the film project as the homegrown one, and both are considered more worthy to the local economy than a host of other electrical workers employed in other industries in the city. At the same time, the "local" association for the gaffers, IATSE 478, has its own geographic codes of meanings. Affiliation requires a presence on local job sites, but not necessarily residency. In order to better serve the studios, the most skilled tradespeople in the film industry live on the move, following nomadic production

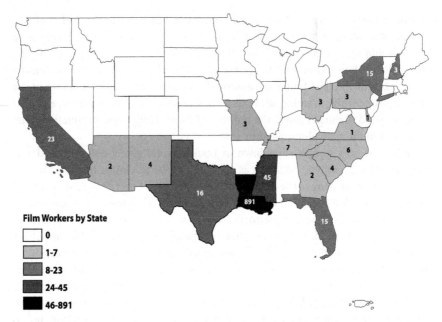

MAP 3. State residencies of film workers who were members of the International Alliance of Theatrical Stage Employees (IATSE), New Orleans local 478, 2007–2012.

crews dispatched from Southern California. Together with the other trade professionals, Louisiana film laborers are designated "Third District" to signify their local base, regardless of where they might crew in the day or sleep at night.

Meanwhile the vernacular meanings of New Orleans as a place and of New Orleanians as a people function in response to their expedient appropriation and exploitation by business and government leaders. Like the roving crews sent in search of filming and studio locations a century ago, film producers visit with a host of cultural assumptions and expectations. They find the city today, as then, a palimpsest defined by decades of successive land and development schemes, the concentration of wealth, and the marketing of authenticity. These perceptions reinforce the liminal status of New Orleanians as alternately cosmopolitan but provincial, loyal but untrustworthy, creative but unproductive, hardworking but unprofessional. One field producer who had relocated to New Orleans a decade ago told me that incoming Hollywood producers more frequently passed over qualified, homegrown talent simply because their local credentials were a stigma. "Out-of-towners love to complain that New Orleanians don't get this or that," she explained, reasoning that no tax benefit offsets the fear of the unknown. "No production wants to get screwed by bad crew; because you're going to end up paying for that in the long run." In sum, the lure of New Orleans as a film place has shortchanged the city's local film workers, treating them as separate and unequal.

Cultural otherness, combined with abysmal political and economic conditions, fuels the aura of Hollywood: an ephemeral and affective sense that a film economy will resolve long-standing social ills and economic disparities. New Orleans in 2014 posted the second-worst income disparity in the United States, putting it on par with the nation of Zambia.[15] The city's privatization strategies, put in place to manage disaster recovery, helped those who already owned homes with more equity, even as wages persistently remained stagnant and decreased in relation to other costs of living. The logic of Disneyomatics has continued to disrupt residents' sense of place by allowing tourism and media industries to identify what is authentic local culture, and who can live sustainably from its marketability. Against these tides that are excavating the stable grounds for a more equal and socially just society, Hollywood South maintains an optimistic front, a fortification based on the fantasy that hardworking individuals, wielding their local pride as a brand, can overcome, in the words of one of the *Treme* fans, "all the things that still need to be fixed."

What has been striking about LFEA's campaigns to retain, if not expand, tax incentives that direct the greatest benefits upward to the richest few is not the absence of these benefactors' faces in campaign representations, but the excess of profiles belonging to the most precarious workers in the regional economy. The biographies of university students and service workers form the basis for the film economy's need for unpaid assistants and underpaid extras in an overall economy of freelancing, temp work, and tip-based gigs. Among them, Susie Labry has personified the "everywoman" in LFEA's efforts. On her website "Louisiana Sunshine," she portrays herself as a background actress with years of short-term gigs as a casting assistant, a typist, a data-entry worker, and a political fund-raiser. Labry came to the foreground on the eve of the 2015 legislative budget debate, creating the "Keep Louisiana Film Industry" Facebook page "to show continued support for Louisiana Film Industry Tax Incentives." Pictures of her at the Capitol and at industry networking sessions—often dressed like a office temp, standing next to a celebrity—have attracted over two thousand followers to her populist and passionate pleas.[16] Like other extras, Labry's performance of herself has been a full-time occupation to maintain the litany of low-to-no-wage gigs that compose her work history.

It's not that Labry and others' hyper-visible politics have amounted to just acting on another stage. These performances are central to film workers' and aspirants' investments in their own career portfolios. To find work, build a network, and then leverage those into the next contract requires film workers to act as entrepreneurs of the self, a disposition of perpetually trading one's image and building one's brand in all spheres of social life. The first rule of becoming a

FIGURE 21. A homeless woman uses the back of a film sign to panhandle near the highway.
Photo by Vicki Mayer.

"power player" in the film industry, assures a manual for entry-level Hollywood
assistants, is to closet your fantasies and remember that the most important person to you is the one you work for.[17] Personalities must be sublimated to this
axiom of career mobility to survive, perhaps forever or until the experience just
feels like being oneself. In a cutthroat industry based on social relationships, the
cruel optimism for little Hollywoods everywhere is not a delusion but a com-
pelled strategy for future achievement. The journalist Barbara Ehrenreich notes:
"As the economy brought more layoffs and financial turbulence to the middle
class, the promoters of positive thinking have increasingly emphasized this negative judgment: to be disappointed, resentful, or downcast is to be a 'victim' and
a 'whiner.'"[18] This lesson is particularly geared to those who live most precariously in film economies. While positive thinking creates the mantra for those
at the top—they are the most meritorious—it disciplines those at the bottom to
fight harder for their dreams.

    The effectiveness of LFEA, and of all film-economy boosterism, lies precisely
in the ways that these populist appeals—to keep sunny-yet-servile attitudes despite economic insecurity—resonate with so much of the U.S. workforce. Once
outliers in the pantheon of labor classifications, the Hollywood model—with its

reliance on the internal competition for short-term, team-based projects—has become the norm throughout much of the post-factory economy. As such, the work routines of the film economy—stressing self-discipline, cooperation, and, above all, communication—are interwoven into the livelihoods of most middle-class Americans.[19] Framed by dismantled and remodeled collective safeguard systems that place more burdens on individuals to fend for themselves, "Precariousness is not an exception; it is rather the rule."[20] To summarize the political theorist Isabell Lorey, precariousness is both an abstract and a concrete form of governance. It demands that workers secure their own education, skills, and training through private debt and negotiate their own contracts for hire, without collective bargaining rights. It places responsibility on individuals to protect themselves from ill or aging bodies, and against harassment or discrimination. The state of insecurity, maintained through passive forms of surveillance and direct policing of the poor, requires that citizens "must perform their exploitable self in multiple social relations before the eyes of others."[21] In this economic context and political climate, Hollywood South becomes an excellent hedge bet because its aura pays so many dividends that the actual labor market does not.

Every time I hear the extraordinary jobs statistics connected to film economies, I am reminded of the security of Hollywood's aura. For the 108 films released by the eleven Hollywood majors in 2013, one study calculated that 84,000 jobs were directly created globally, with more than 13,500 located in Louisiana.[22] Add to that the production projects for television, advertising, special events, and digital media, and the industry touts creating another 11,000 jobs annually in the state.[23] These are the fruits of the film economy, the ones that justify starving other state spending priorities. They are temporary. Many film jobs last only a day. They are unstable. Film jobs flourish where they receive the most subsidy, often in right-to-work states that erode the power of the industry's own labor unions and professional guilds. Few people make their sole living in the role of a film and television worker. Yet film jobs are also aspirational. For LFEA's claim that one in ten Louisianans are employed or know someone who is employed by the film industry to be correct, it would *have* to include the multitudes of workers who are only vicariously connected to Hollywood. Technocrats call these people the "multiplier effects" of film economies, but they are actually the middle-class people in my own social milieu who are struggling to make ends meet.

From the college student who bags groceries to pay for film classes in the hopes of being a director, to the professor incentivized to teach less film theory and more production skills, so powerful is the aura of Hollywood that any political critique becomes impossibly personalized through the network of people connecting themselves to it. After fifteen years, the dream of Hollywood South has deep roots in my own community of friends, neighbors, and colleagues. Even my boyfriend, a highly educated scientist, counted our mutual friend as a "film industry worker" despite the fact that this person worked full-time as a legal secretary, and only occasionally as an extra. By the same token, this contigent film worker, an otherwise-critical thinker, promotes the film economy unquestioningly—and for good reason. He can pay his mortgage only by renting half his house to a stream of visiting film professionals. The feelings of precariousness, the real danger of slipping into poverty, and the sense that we willingly participate in this political economy make it hard not to cheer on the film industry or become a foot solider to its craven needs. Those who question the policy's means or ends, including myself, must defend against charges of rudeness, elitism, or even callousness to the plight of fellow citizens. To parallel film financing to the subsequent cuts to education and health services becomes heretical. Therein lies the rub for eliminating policies that underwrite Hollywood South and all of its competitors elsewhere.

WHY ZOMBIES CAN DISSENT

To resist the mandatory optimism, many New Orleanians have resorted to either ambivalence or cynicism toward the film economy. Annual Mardi Gras parade floats have lampooned the eye-popping corruption scandals, and the fawning reverence for celebrities, and the absurd marketing of everything shot in New Orleans, regardless of whether or not it is any good. These tactics do little to assuage our discomfort, the sense of the *unheimlich,* on the other, less eventful days of the year, such as when the fleet of Hollywood trucks blocks the streets, the parks, and our passage. Much less do these carnivalesque critiques form, on their own, a coherent politics for a creative economy in the future.

What is the mojo against the zombie kings, vampires, and all other lords of the underworld that shroud their black magic in the promises of creative freedoms, job creation, and local returns on investment? Interestingly, LFEA's own research—the study promised as the reward of the Two Bucks Campaign— perhaps contains the antidote to the bad economic policies the industry peddles. Released with great fanfare during the legislative budgeting process, the study combined the findings of two telephone surveys asking residents and tourists, respectively, how they *feel* about Hollywood South. Among the former sample, 80 percent of Louisianans wanted a film economy, but only half wanted the tax incentive policy. Among the latter group of some 1,400 recent tourists to Louisiana, only about 200 of them said that a film made in Louisiana was one of the reasons they came to visit. Many more could name a film or television show located in the state. They include, prominently, *A Streetcar Named Desire* (1951), *The Big Easy* (1986), *Interview with the Vampire* (1994), and *Steel Magnolias* (1989). Most of these are set in New Orleans, but all of them were produced well before the political institutionalization of Hollywood South.[24] What the two studies together

FIGURE 22. A sign on a 2016 Mardi Gras float lampoons the political characters in the budget-ary drama surrounding the state's film tax-credit policy. Photo by Vicki Mayer.

reveal are not the resounding cheers of the masses for the current policies, but a more complex swirl of feelings supporting the people and places that have created New Orleans as a place of creative people.

Those feelings of identification and solidarity need to be captured in a public sphere that presents the current film incentive policies for what they are and who they are designed to serve. Writing against the financialization of all values in the postindustrial society, social theorist Franco Berardi has advocated a collective intelligence that imagines "a place we do not know" based on mutual connections and empathy.[25] He cites the autonomous and horizontal social movements that have brought together artists, journalists, programmers, and computer techni-cians to subvert market logics with irony, an act that exposes the fault lines in the law. These groups, such as Wikileaks, Anonymous, the Debt Collective, and Oc-cupy, among others, use irony as a way to reveal the opaque circulation of capital and power among those who act above the laws they enforce on others. They re-fuse to play by all the rules of the game or to obey legal directives that try to control people through sustained relations of precarity. Rather than opting for cynicism, however, "Ironic interpretations of events presuppose a common understanding between the speakers and the listeners; a sympathy among those who, engaged in the ironic act, arrive at a common autonomy from the dictatorship of the signi-fied."[26] In other words, this new place that Berardi imagines is a temporal one, based on open dialogue, transparent information access, and the possibility of as many interpretations as there are discussants. This seems like an excellent place to begin a more open and sustained discussion about the multitude of relationships between creativity and economy.

Berardi's vision reminds me of the homemade signs after Katrina that called on us to "Think You Might Be Wrong" without disclosing the original sin. The fact that most New Orleanians have no idea where the money for film incentives comes from in the budget, or into whose pockets it goes, signifies a deep chasm to cross if anyone is to have faith in a well-governed creative economy that benefits everyone. The policy propping up Hollywood South has diverted attention away from the real beneficiaries of film and other entertainment incentive policies: from the project investors who offload their risks onto precarious workers, to developer magnates who use public monies to turn blighted properties into private gold, to the small cabal of legal and financial professionals who both oversee and profit from the tradable-tax-credit market that few know exists and even fewer enter. New solutions need to overcome the false binary of the deserving creative worker and the undeserving ordinary citizen, and to avoid recreating a trickle-down economy between the direct beneficiaries of the subsidies and those relegated to the minimum-wage margins as a result of the policy's multiplier effects. If this book contributes anything to the possibility of seeing film economies through their obscurantist language and false dichotomies, then at least we can begin again.

From there, we can collectively restore the senses of the local that everyone—from the affluent visitor in the LFEA survey to the struggling extras trying to make the skyrocketing rents and even the die-hard media fans in between—articulates in their visions of a local place with local laborers. What might be done with the collected tax moneys that have been sheltered in film-studio investments or redistributed via the credit brokers? Could we imagine a city in which workers are not dependent on unreliable tips, substandard wages, or the largesse of elite patrons? The organizing efforts to double the base floor of the minimum wages and provide basic services for all workers, including restaurant servers, musicians, and street performers, helps everyone rise in the struggles for economic justice.[27] Health and education need to respond not only to private industry's needs, but also to crazy work schedules and locational mobility without incurring unsustainable debt loads. In Louisiana, Medicaid is still out of reach for most people working full-time. The local public university system has shrunk to a shadow of its former self, declaring financial exigency in the face of the population returning to its pre-Katrina size.[28] Rent controls and free access to expanded transportation or equipment rentals can offset the excesses of the marketplace and restore the small social contracts that residents have with public space, their neighborhoods, and their neighbors. Those goods could become fully embedded in the community with credit waivers for subsidized housing, fairer pricing for flood insurance, and access to nearby public spaces for work studios, community resource centers, and media making. This final idea would reinforce that a creative economy policy needs to be transparent, multivoiced, and subject to public scrutiny, irony, and a dynamic circuit for responses.[29]

Some regional and city governments have begun thinking about their local creative economies in ways that bring together constituencies' concerns for complex solidarities. Minnesota in 2008 passed a constitutional amendment that dedicated tax funding to arts, clean water, and parks. The yoking of arts and environment (as a shared public investment) with protection of public spaces and infrastructure in the creation of art is one path forward. Another avenue is to think through possible ways to redistribute wealth downward. Missouri in 2015 collected $42 million in income taxes on their nonresident Hollywood entertainers and pro athletes to support the state arts council. Finally, there are local policies to tie education and creative arts funding. In Portland, Oregon, the citywide Arts Education and Access Fund overrides unequal education policies based on property values and fosters funding to make creative arts a universal right for youth. While the measure that supports the fund since 2012 has had multiple opponents and revisions, the overall focus on grassroots efforts to stimulate *all* people's creative potentials is a step in the right direction.[30]

Rather than wishing for a superhero to fight the lords of zombies and the scions of vampires, the tragic outcomes of Hollywood South might be countered with a Hall of Justice for all people as creative and as workers. This would involve extending local film-labor advantages to all local workers, regardless of industry or trade, status or documentation. It would require reinvesting in the educational, health, and retirement programs that would uplift all workers. It would allow employers to capitalize on the full range of local expertise and create a secure resource in a time of continuing crisis elsewhere. Most importantly, it would put the public back in the dyad of the public–private partnerships that were supposed to build a more creative, if not a more just, society.

A Guide to Decoding Film Economy Claims and Press Coverage

Newspaper coverage of the film industry has been based largely on economic research and reports generated by firms cozy with the benefactors of the tax incentives. In Louisiana, Loren C. Scott and Associates has prepared a yearly assessment of the regional tax credit policies for the Louisiana Department of Economic Development, which administers the program. A consultant for energy, oil, and gas and a number of large banks, the economist Dr. Scott has favored tax breaks, opposes labor unions, and warns against all forms of government regulation as a general economic principle.[1] Yet his group's last economic analysis of the film tax-credit program received a lukewarm reception from the LFEA and the MPAA for *under*estimating the positive effects of the incentives. They, in turn, issued a counter-report with their own figures.[2] From there, newspapers balanced the findings of these reports as a narrow debate between dueling econometric formulas. The larger questions about film economy policy are left in the hands of the technocrats.

How should we as citizens understand this "inside baseball" of film policy? While this book is largely a cultural analysis of a regional film economy, it is not so difficult to read through the various editions of the policy and its optimistic analyses. Without even knowing the ways the projections are calculated, citizens can decode the variety of expert-driven reports and their assumptions with just a few rhetorical tools.

To exemplify, I offer my own close reading of a 2013 report by Scott and Associates, "The Economic Impact of Louisiana's Entertainment Tax Credit Programs," which touts the slew of entertainment tax-credit programs for clearly resulting in "increased business sales and jobs for Louisiana residents" up through 2012.[3] The devilishness of the statement is clearly in the details, particularly in how we define *sales* and *jobs* and then how these outputs compare to the state's basic expenditures. Even as many aspects of the policy have changed how the numbers will add up for 2016–17, the basic assumptions around how the state defines business sales and film jobs are the foundation upon which all the other calculations rest.

Beginning with business sales, the state certified approximately $717.2 million in film-production spending in Louisiana by Hollywood studios in 2012. Another $18 million or so was certified for building Louisiana film infrastructure, though this was most likely not initiated by studios. The first figure, though, is taken as the baseline for business sales, since the certification is to verify that the studios spent that money in state. However, money spent in state does not mean that the business itself is Louisiana based. Indeed spending on hotel chains and airline companies may originate in state, but the profit margins flow outward to corporate headquarters elsewhere. Fees associated with bonds and financing are also included as business sales, though arguably most people would associate fees with a negative penalty on studios, and not a positive sale. To this figure of $717.2 million, the report's authors add another $316.9 million in indirect business sales. Indirect sales are estimates of how many business sales might be related to a direct sale in film production. For example, if a film crew stays in a hotel and the hotel has to hire more staff or supplies, these would be considered positive business sales for the film economy.

The report uses a literary metaphor to justify its fuzzy math: "When the rock [of direct spending] hits the pond, it will send ripple effects all the way to the edge of the pond. These ripples are what economists refer to as indirect or multiplier effects of the entertainment spending."[4] This is a rather elegant image for what critics say is, in reality, "no science, and it may be stretching things to call it an art."[5] Using an input/output table developed by the U.S. Bureau of Labor Statistics, the multipliers for film production are fundamentally grounded in a common interest between state film commissions and the film industry to promote regional economic impacts. For Louisiana, this art of the multipliers allows the state to estimate that film production resulted in just over $1 billion in business sales in 2012. If the report's authors wanted to give a more accurate picture of business sales, it would take the direct certified sales, subtract any spending on businesses not based in Louisiana, and then subtract the tax credits that, in effect, gave the money back to the studios. In 2012, this rebate was $218.4 million, bringing the direct business sales down to less than $500 million to begin with. While this figure implies that for every $1 the state spends, film studios spend about $2 in state, this impact is far smaller than that of other industries, especially those that would rely entirely on Louisiana-based resources, whether that is lumber or labor.

As for the second term in that pairing, *labor*, the jobs impact in the report has to be qualified with the precious notion of what is a job. I would hazard that most people, when presented with numbers of jobs, imagine regular employment, either in a stable position or in an actual place. Neither of these assumptions applies to the "jobs" cited in the report by Scott. Film jobs are contract work, most referring to employment for a limited time, anywhere from three months to only a day. A single worker may then occupy up to ten jobs in a given calendar year. To illustrate a correlative jobs number in New Orleans would mean counting the number of music jobs created by clubs by counting the aggregate total of musicians who play in gigs each night for a year. The temporary nature of the industry's presence in state means that the average film worker must piece together various jobs over the course of a year, frequently working second or third jobs that can ensure more stable sources of income. In the United States, film jobs are most sustainable in regions where other core entertainment industries are located, namely Southern California and New York City.

With this considerable caveat in mind, the report claims that the film industry created 5,976 jobs directly, along with another 8,329 indirectly, in 2012. Together, these jobs were said to generate $717.9 million in household earnings. The direct jobs are simply the total number of workers that were qualified to receive a tax credit as a hire, regardless of whether the hire was a Louisiana resident. The indirect jobs were figured using another estimate based on census data for all jobs that could be associated with film production. These occupations include miners, farmers, and real estate agents; the latter, coincidentally, had the most jobs added to their ranks in 2012—828 realtors were presumed to be employed thanks to film-production multipliers.[6] The aggregate earnings of the indirect jobs were similarly based on the total of average wages in those professions. Hence, the film industry was reported to be responsible for 1,152 extra health-care workers, such as paramedics and nurses, who make relatively good earnings ($46.3 million), but also for 581 extra food servers making relatively poor earnings ($10 million). In both cases, however, the correlation with film production is largely imagined—based on the idea that film workers are somehow different from other workers in the economy. Most tellingly, the report asserts that film production's economic impacts need to include these indirect estimates, because

> When workers in the industry receive their paychecks, they will then take that money and spend some of it at grocery stores, car dealerships, clothing stores, theaters, etc., in the state. This creates new incomes for people in those sectors, and they will go spend their earnings at grocery stores, car dealerships, clothing stores, theaters, etc., and the cycle keeps repeating.[7]

By this definition, every worker would have a multiplier effect, and some workers would have far bigger ripples than the film worker. To wit, the report cites only the direct employment and earnings figures for workers in Louisiana's paper industry and transportation-equipment manufacturing sectors; both dwarf the direct figures for film production, and the jobs in those sectors are presumably more regular for the individuals employed in them.

All of this begs the question why the state goes to such trouble to obscure the economic impacts of the film-production tax credit with so many uncertain numbers and dubious calculations. The answer to this question is not only economic, but also cultural. The final calculation that is a key to the report is the average wage supposedly earned by workers affected by the film industry. This figure, which averages the aggregate earnings of each sector directly and indirectly employed by the film industry, comes to $51,239 annually, a figure that seems to tower over the average earnings of most Louisianians.[8] From this, we see the class conceit about creative workers: they earn more and thus spend more. Their consumption will drive an economy associated with overpriced loft living, bourgeois services, and conspicuous spending habits. Unfortunately, even this number is a fiction. The average-wage calculation includes the highest-paid individuals in film production, such as starring actors and actresses, directors, and producers. The fact that those few individuals who earn millions per film project (and who largely do not live in Louisiana) cannot be disaggregated from the payrolls for these calculations should remind residents, first, that their labor also earns the studio at least a 30 percent tax credit; and, second, that these privileged few workers offset the annual wages of the thousands below them who work for minimum wage. The wage realities of the masses of workers affected by the film industry are thus completely invisible in the state's rosy assessment.

NOTES

INTRODUCTION

1. See Film L.A. Inc., "2013 Feature Film Production Report," Film L.A. Research, accessed July 1, 2014, http://www.filmla.com/data_reports.php. Corresponding coverage can be found in Monica Hernandez, "Louisiana Has Become the World's Film Production Capitol, Report Says," WWLTV.com, March 1, 2014, accessed July 1, 2014, http://www.wwltv.com/news/Louisiana-has-become-worlds-film-production-capitol-report-says-249667371.html; and Mike Scott, "Movie Magnet—La. Is the Film Production Capital of the World, Study Finds," *The Times-Picayune,* March 12, 2014, C1.

2. These figures are drawn from 2012 U.S. census data.

3. Revenues drawn from the 2010–12 totals presented in the state's commissioned report: Loren C. Scott & Associates, Inc., "The Economic Impact of Louisiana's Entertainment Tax Credit Programs," report for the Office of Entertainment Industry Development, Louisiana Department of Economic Development, April 2013, accessed May 1, 2014, http://louisianaentertainment.gov/docs/main/2013_OEID_Program_Impact_Report_(FINAL).pdf. Budget shortfalls are documented in the *Times-Picayune* over the same period.

4. Gordon Russell, "Special Report: How Startling, Unique Cuts Have Transformed Louisiana's Universities," *The Advocate,* January 23, 2016, accessed January 27, 2016, http://theadvocate.com/news/14621878-123/special-report-how-startling-unique-cuts-have-transformed-louisianas-universities.

5. "Bobby Jindal's Louisiana Prioritizes Tax Cuts over Child Safety," *Daily Kos,* April 15, 2014, accessed September 9, 2014, http://www.dailykos.com/story/2014/04/15/1292153/-Bobby-Jindal-s-Louisiana-Prioritizes-tax-cuts-over-child-safety#.

6. See a summary and critique of these images in Diane Negra, ed., *Old and New Media after Katrina* (London: Palgrave, 2010).

7. The concept of crisis ordinariness is drawn from Lauren Berlant, *Cruel Optimism* (Durham, NC: Duke University Press, 2011), 101–5.

8. Michael Cieply, "Hollywood Begs for a Tax Break in Some States, Including California," *The New York Times,* April 17, 2012, accessed July 17, 2014, http://www.nytimes.com/2014/04/18/business/media/hollywood-begs-for-a-tax-break-in-some-states-including-california.html?_r = 0.

9. For example, see Colin Brown, "Independent Film as an Attractive Asset Class," white paper for *Filmnomics,* November 2012, accessed July 17, 2014, http://info.slated.com; and Robert Tannenwald, "State Film Subsidies: Not Much Bang for Too Many Bucks," Center on Budget and Policy Priorities, November 17, 2010, accessed November 20, 2010, http://www.cbpp.org/research/state-film-subsidies-not-much-bang-for-too-many-bucks.

10. Joseph Henchman, "Motion Picture Association Attacks Tax Foundation Critique of Film Subsidies," *States News Service,* June 29, 2011, accessed June 13, 2012, http://taxfoundation.org/article/motion-picture-association-attacks-tax-foundation-critique-film-tax-subsidies.

11. The original essay can be found in Sigmund Freud, *The Uncanny* (London: Penguin, 2003), with an extension about meanings of the uncanny and home in Homi Bhabha, *The Location of Culture* (London: Routledge, 2007).

12. Matt Sakakeeny, "Privatization, Marketization, and Neoliberalism: The Political Dynamics of Post-Katrina New Orleans," *Perspectives on Politics* 10 (2012): 723–6.

13. The rewriting of Los Angeles history into Hollywood's mythical origins is recounted in a recent spate of cultural histories, especially Vincent Brook, *Land of Smoke and Mirrors: A Cultural History of Los Angeles* (New Brunswick, NJ: Rutgers University Press, 2013); Leo Braudy, *The Hollywood Sign: Fantasy and Reality of an American Icon* (New Haven, CT: Yale University Press); Jan Olsson, *Los Angeles before Hollywood: Journalism and American Film Culture* (Stockholm: National Library of Sweden, 2008); and Mark Shiel, *Hollywood Cinema and the Real Los Angeles* (London: Reaktion Books, 2012). The laws of agglomeration and the self-perpetuation of film-production clusters are particular to economic geography. To read more on Hollywood in particular, see Michael Storper, *Keys to the City: How Economics, Institutions, Social Interaction, and Politics Shape Development* (Princeton, NJ: Princeton University Press, 2013); and Allen Scott, *On Hollywood: The Place, the Industry* (Princeton, NJ: Princeton University Press, 2005).

14. Braudy, *The Hollywood Sign,* 11–2.

15. Toby Miller, Nitin Govil, John McMurria, Richard Maxwell, and Ting Wang, *Global Hollywood 2* (London: BFI, 2005), 127.

16. Shiel, *Hollywood Cinema and the Real Los Angeles,* 26–30.

17. This is characterized by Aida Hozic as the triumph of time efficiencies over spatial mobilities in *Hollyworld: Space, Power and Fantasy in the American Economy* (Ithaca, NY: Cornell University Press, 2001), 93.

18. Andrew Erish, *Col. William Selig, the Man Who Invented Hollywood* (Austin: University of Texas Press, 2012), 131.

19. Neil Coe and Jennifer Johns, "Beyond Production Clusters: Towards a Critical Political Economy of Networks in the Film and Television Industries," in *The Cultural Industries and the Production of Culture,* eds. Dominic Power and Allen Scott (London: Routledge, 2011), 188–204.

20. This has the added side effect of creating greater segmentation between workers who do not fit into the cultural network. See Susan Christopherson, "Beyond the Self-Expressive

Creative Worker: An Industry Perspective on Entertainment Media," *Theory, Culture & Society* 25 (2008): 73–95.

21. Much of this story is recounted in Miller et al., *Global Hollywood 2*, 61–4. One other point worth remembering, though, is the push and pull between the different government and industry players at this time. See, for example, W. D. Phillips, "'A Maze of Intricate Relationships': Mae D. Huettig and Early Forays into Film Industry Studies," *Film History* 27 (2015): 135–63.

22. Thomas Schatz, *The Genius of the System: Hollywood Filmmaking in the Studio Era* (Austin: University of Texas, 1988).

23. Erish, *Col. William Selig*, 213–7.

24. The best overview of Hollywood's monopolistic practices, including its vertical integration, block booking, and blind-buying contracts, is in Mae D. Huettig, *Economic Control of the Motion Picture Industry: A Study in Industrial Organization* (Philadelphia: University of Pennsylvania Press, 1944).

25. This story about the era after *Paramount* is also recounted in many places, including Justin Wyatt, *High Concept: Movies and Marketing in Hollywood* (Austin: University of Texas Press, 1994); and Jennifer Holt, *Empires of Entertainment: Media Industries and the Politics of Deregulation, 1980–1996* (New Brunswick, NJ: Rutgers University Press, 2011).

26. Brian Taves, "The B-Film: Hollywood's Other Half," in *Grand Design: Hollywood as a Modern Business Enterprise, 1930–1939*, ed. Tino Balio (Berkeley: University of California Press, 1995), 321.

27. Shooting schedules were printed in the trade magazine *Motion Picture Daily*.

28. Todd Platts, "The Undead of Hollywood and Poverty Row: The Influence of Studio-Era Industrial Patterns on Zombie Film Production, 1932–1946," in *Merchants of Menace: The Business of Horror Cinema*, ed. Richard Nowell (New York: Bloomsbury, 2014), 31–44.

29. Platts, "The Undead of Hollywood and Poverty Row," 39.

30. Michael Storper and Susan Christopherson, "Flexible Specialization and Regional Industrial Agglomerations: The Case of the U.S. Motion Picture Industry," *Annals of the Association of American Geographers* 77 (1987): 104–17.

31. Toby Miller and Marie Claire Leger, "Runaway Production, Runaway Consumption, Runaway Citizenship: The New International Division of Cultural Labor," *Emergences* 11 (2001): 89–115.

32. S. Frederick Starr, "Introduction: The Man Who Invented New Orleans," in *Inventing New Orleans: The Writings of Lafcadio Hearn*, ed. S. Frederick Starr (Jackson: University of Mississippi Press, 2001), xii.

33. Ned Sublette, *The World That Made New Orleans: From Spanish Silver to Congo Square* (Chicago: Lawrence Hill Books, 2008), 285.

34. Information about the geography of New Orleans's theater district was compiled from city directories for 1900–07 and supplemented by Will Branan, "Movies: The Little Sister of 'Legit' and 'Vodvil,'" *The Daily Picayune*, July 21, 1912, 31. The directories did not include nickelodeons, which would have been an attraction for working-class audiences. Early Louisiana cinema history has been gathered in a variety of sources, including Ed Poole and Susan Poole, *Louisiana Film History: The First Hundred Years (1896–1996)* (Harvey, LA: Learn About Network, 2012); and the archival website http://medianola.org.

35. A set of recent cultural histories tells of New Orleans's manufacture and sale of its authenticity to benefit local elites through tourism and cultural industries. My personal favorites are John Shelton Reed, *Dixie Bohemia: A French Quarter Circle in the 1920s* (Baton Rouge, LA: LSU Press, 2012); J. Mark Souther, *New Orleans on Parade: Tourism and the Transformation of the Crescent City* (Baton Rouge, LA: LSU Press, 2013); and Lynnell Thomas, *Desire and Disaster in New Orleans: Tourism, Race, and Historical Memory* (Durham, NC: Duke University Press, 2014).

36. Richard Campanella, *Bienville's Dilemma: A Historical Geography of New Orleans* (Lafayette: University of Louisiana at Lafayette, 2008), 175–6, 188.

37. Souther, *New Orleans on Parade*, 41.

38. Thomas, *Desire and Disaster*, 28.

39. This aggregate number of shooting locations comes via Poole and Poole, *Louisiana Film History*.

40. State Science and Technology Institute, "Louisiana Vision Plan 2020: Action Plan 2001," report for the Louisiana Economic Development Council, Baton Rouge, January 2001, accessed July 10, 2008, http://ssti.org/blog/louisiana-vision-2020-action-plan-2001.

41. Brett Clanton, "Louisiana's Arts and Entertainment Director Works to Attract Film Industry," *New Orleans City Business News*, November 5, 2001, accessed January 27, 2016, http://www.lexisnexis.com/hottopics/lnacademic.

42. This history is better plotted in a larger literature about film production economics, including Storper and Christopherson, "Flexible Specialization and Regional Industrial Agglomerations"; Asu Askoy and Kevin Robins, "Hollywood for the 21st Century: Global Competition for Critical Mass in Image Markets," *Cambridge Journal of Economics* 16 (1992): 1–22; Susan Christopherson and Michael Storper, "The City as Studio; the World as Back Lot: The Impact of Vertical Disintegration on the Location of the Major Motion Picture Industry," *Environment and Planning D: Society and Space* 4 (1986): 305–20; Mike Gasher, *Hollywood North: The Feature Film Industry in British Columbia* (Vancouver: UBC Press, 2002); Serra Tinic, *On Location: Canada's Television Industry in a Global Market* (Buffalo, NY: SUNY Press, 2005); Susan Christopherson and Ned Rightor, "The Creative Economy as 'Big Business': Evaluating State Strategies to Lure Film Makers," *Journal of Planning, Education and Research* 29 (2010): 336–52.

43. Susan Christopherson and Jennifer Clark, *Remaking Regional Economies: Power, Labor and Firm Strategies in the Knowledge Economy* (London: Routledge, 2009), 11.

44. Loren C. Scott and James A. Richardson, "The Louisiana Economic Outlook: 2014 and 2015," report for the Division of Economic Development, E.J. Ourso College of Business, Louisiana State University, October 2013, accessed July 18, 2014, http://www.daily-review.com/sites/default/files/DR%20LOREN%20SCOTT_LEO%202014-15.pdf. Scott's firm, coincidentally, also audits and provides the economic analysis of film incentives in the state.

45. Brett Clanton, "Legislature May Help Get Films Rolling in LA," *New Orleans City Business News*, March 25, 2002, accessed January 27, 2016, http://www.lexisnexis.com/hottopics/lnacademic.

46. Will Luther, "Movie Production Incentives & Film Tax Credits: Blockbuster Support for Lackluster Policy," *The Tax Foundation*, January 14, 2010, accessed July 20, 2014, http://taxfoundation.org/article/movie-production-incentives-film-tax-credits-blockbuster-support-lackluster-policy.

47. Christopherson and Rightor, "The Creative Economy," 338–9. This was shown most recently in a widely publicized power struggle between the state of Maryland and the Netflix producers for *House of Cards* (cf. Timothy B. Wheeler and David Zurawik, "Tax Breaks for *House of Cards* Fall Short," *Baltimore Sun,* April 8, 2014, accessed January 27, 2016, http://www.baltimoresun.com/news/maryland/politics/blog/bs-md-film-credit-aftermath-20140408-story.html).

48. These assertions are based on the steady tracking of online rankings made over the years by the film-tax-credit brokerage house Film Production Capital (http://filmproduction capital.com) and news coverage of state poverty indices and film policies. See also Zach Patton, "The Value of Movie Tax Incentives," *Governing,* June 2010, accessed July 17, 2014, http://www.governing.com/topics/economic-dev/The-Value-of-Movie-Tax-Incentives.html; and Louise Story, "Michigan Town Woos Hollywood, but Ends Up with a Bit Part," *The New York Times,* December 4, 2012, A1, A18.

49. This is from the standpoint that the state subsidizes an industry that pays no direct taxes and is true of all tax incentive programs. In most cases, however, the losses incurred in a given year would be made up by the stable new industry in that location eventually. This is not the case with a highly mobile production process, such as location shooting. See Tim Mathis, "Louisiana Film Tax Credits: Selling Out to Hollywood," *Louisiana Budget Project,* November 22, 2010, accessed January 27, 2016, http://www.labudget.org/lbp/2010/11/louisiana-film-tax-credits-selling-out-to-hollywood/.

50. Cieply, Michael, "Jitters Are Setting In for States Giving Big Incentives to Lure Film Producers," *The New York Times,* October 12, 2008, 26.

51. Mount Auburn and Associates, "Louisiana: Where Culture Means Business," report prepared for the Office of Cultural Development/Louisiana Division of the Arts, Office of the Lieutenant Governor, 3–4, July 31, 2005, accessed January 27, 2016, http://www.crt.state.la.us/Assets/OCD/arts/culturedistricts/reports/cultureeconomyreport.pdf. Emphasis in quote is mine.

52. Stacey Plaisance, "Louisiana Sees Surge in TV & Film Projects," *Associated Press State & Local Newswire,* December 2, 2011, accessed June 13, 2012, http://www.wwltv.com/story/news/2014/08/29/14415654/; Mike Scott, "Louisiana Film Industry Passes Billion-Dollar Mark in Record-Setting 2011," *The Times-Picayune,* January 7, 2011, accessed June 13, 2012, http://www.nola.com/movies/index.ssf/2012/01/louisiana_film_industry_passes.html.

53. This term is generally associated with Richard Florida, an economic-sociologist-cum-urban-development-consultant, via his classic text *The Rise of the Creative Class: And How It's Transforming Work, Leisure, Community and Everyday Life* (New York: Perseus Books, 2002).

54. "Louisiana Department of Economic Development Strategic Plan 2009–2013," Louisiana Economic Development Council, Baton Rouge, 2008, accessed September 1, 2014, http://archive.thetowntalk.com/assets/pdf/DK1226071117.pdf.

55. The Creative Class Group, which advocated creative economy building based on research by its founder Richard Florida, has now taken a turn to critique the inequality generated by creative economy policies. See, for example, Richard Florida, "S.F.'s Dilemma: Boom Is Pushing Out Those Who Make It Desirable," *SF Gate,* September 30, 2014, accessed January 27, 2016, http://www.sfgate.com/opinion/openforum/article/S-F-s-dilemma-boom-is-pushing-out-those-who-5792382.php.

56. Greg Hernandez, "La's Hollywood Dreams Are Dashed by Katrina," *The Philadelphia Inquirer,* September 4, 2005, H4; Joel High, "Movie, Music Industries Must Commit to Aid," *Billboard.com,* September 17, 2005, 4; Bashirah Muttalib, "Shreveport Lures Prod'n," *Variety,* July 24, 2007, 13; Kelly Anderson, "TV Rising in New Orleans," *Realscreen,* March 1, 2008, 8.

57. Mike Scott, "A Star Is Reborn: Hollywood South Bounces Back from the Storm," *Nola.com,* October 6, 2007, accessed September 13, 2012, http://www.nola.com/movies/index.ssf/2007/10/a_star_is_reborn_hollywood_sou.html.

58. Lewis Simpson quoted in Reed, *Dixie Bohemia,* 57.

59. Christopherson and Clark, *Remaking Regional Economies,* 12.

CHAPTER 1. THE MAKING OF REGIONAL FILM ECONOMIES: WHY LA. IS NOT L.A.

1. Scott Ellis, *Madame Vieux Carré* (Baton Rouge, LA: LSU Press, 2010), 12; see also Germaine A. Reed, "Race Legislation in Louisiana, 1864–1920," *Louisiana History: The Journal of the Louisiana Historical Association* 6 (1965): 379–92.

2. City directories for 1900–07, supplemented with Branan, "Movies: The Little Sister of 'Legit' and 'Vodvil,'" *The Daily Picayune,* July 21, 1912, 31. The directories did not include nickelodeons, which would have been an attraction for working-class audiences.

3. "Lyric's Season," *The Daily Picayune,* August 14, 1905, 4.

4. Ari Kelman, *A River and Its City: The Nature of Landscape in New Orleans, with a New Preface* (Berkeley: University of California Press, 2006), 150–5.

5. *Insurance Maps of New Orleans, Volume 2* (New York: Sandborn Map Company, 1908), sheets 185 and 192; and Darlene M. Walk, ed., *Bayou St. John Profile* (New Orleans: City of New Orleans, 1979), 3.04.

6. The new neighborhoods of Jockey Club, Fontainebleau, and Carrollton were also mentioned in "Real Estate the Real Thing Here," *The Daily Picayune,* September 1, 1912, 40. The parceling of the lands lakeside of the bayou can be tracked in the newspaper throughout the period.

7. The "good roads" moniker is cited in Robert W. Williams, Jr., *Martin Behrman: Mayor and Political Boss of New Orleans, 1904–1926* (master's thesis, Tulane University, 1952), 156. The latter quote is from an address to the New Orleans Sewage and Water Board in 1914, cited in Kelman, *A River and Its City,* 155.

8. Building permits alone brought more than $5 million to the budget in 1905, approximately twenty times their value from the previous year, according to John Kendall, *History of New Orleans* (Chicago: Lewis, 1922), 555.

9. "Selig Notes," *The Moving Picture World* 6 (1910): 341.

10. "Picturing the City," *The Daily Picayune,* January 12, 1909, 5. The series of film shorts can be found on page 10 of Selig's 1903 catalog, which is part of the American Film Institute's online database, accessed July 16, 2013, http://afi.chadwyck.com.

11. From 1907 to 1914, White City Amusement Park was located on what today is the corner of Tulane and Carrollton avenues. A baseball park replaced it. Leonard V. Huber, *New Orleans: A Pictorial History* (New York: Crown, 1971), 239.

12. J. S. McQuade, "The Los Angeles Tragedy," *The Moving Picture World* 10 (1911): 455; "Interesting Sidelights on Character of Motion Picture Pioneer of the West," *San Jose*

Mercury News, December 12, 1915, 165; "Selig: The Man Behind Boggs, Responsible for Calif. Studios," *Motography* 14 (1915): 560; Jas McQuade, "Chicago Letter," *The Moving Picture World* 26 (1915): 1979.

13. Andrew Erish, *Col. William Selig, the Man Who Invented Hollywood* (Austin: University of Texas Press, 2012), 20, 30; Scott Curtis, "A House Divided: The MPPC in Transition," in *American Cinema's Transitional Era: Audiences, Institutions, Practices,* eds. Charlie Keil and Shelley Stamp (Berkeley: University of California Press, 2004), 245; "National Independent Moving Picture Alliance," *The Moving Picture World* 5 (1909): 410; "Uncle Sam—Inquisitor," *The Moving Picture World* 15 (1913): 551.

14. This is a slightly ironic twist on film scholars' argument that early filmmakers fled to Los Angeles to escape the power of the Edison Trust on the East Coast. Given that Selig was a member of the trust, it could be that trust members wanted to insulate themselves from independent distributors.

15. The perception of economic risk is indeed a textbook concept in any management psychology primer. See, for example, Francis X. Diebold, Neil A. Doherty, and Richard J. Herring, *The Known, the Unknown, and the Unknowable in Financial Risk Management: Measurement and Theory Advancing Practice* (Princeton, NJ: Princeton University Press, 2010).

16. Michael Storper, *Keys to the City: How Economics, Institutions, Social Interaction, and Politics Shape Development* (Princeton, NJ: Princeton University Press, 2013), 72. His extended argument about the cultural factors that drive different kinds of innovation economies is found in chapters 10 and 11 of the same book.

17. Ibid., 160.

18. Janet Staiger, "The Director-Unit System: Management of Multiple Unit Companies after 1909," in *The Classical Hollywood Cinema: Film Style and Mode of Production to 1960,* eds. David Bordwell, Janet Staiger, and Kristin Thompson (New York: Columbia University Press, 1985), 121–7.

19. Mark Shiel, *Hollywood Cinema and the Real Los Angeles* (London: Reaktion Books, 2012), 21–2.

20. Hillary Hallett, *Go West, Young Women! The Rise of Early Hollywood* (Berkeley: University of California Press, 2013); and Vincent Brook, "The Ramona Myth," in *Land of Smoke and Mirrors: A Cultural History of Los Angeles* (New Brunswick, NJ: Rutgers University Press, 2013), 25–42.

21. "Sixth Kalem Company at New Orleans," *The Moving Picture World* 11 (1912): 309; "Studio Saunterings," *The Moving Picture World* 13 (1912): 26.

22. "Marion Optimistic," *The Moving Picture World* 11 (1912): 1052; "News and Notables at the New Orleans Hotels," *The Daily Picayune,* February, 28, 1912, 7.

23. "Le Soir Back from New Orleans," *The Moving Picture World* 12 (1912): 639. Poole and Poole arrive at the same conclusions in *Louisiana Film History: The First Hundred Years (1896–1996)* (Harvey, LA: Learn About Network, 2012), 22.

24. Allen Scott, "Cultural Economy and the Creative Field of the City," *Geografiska Annaler, Series B: Human Geography* 90 (2010): 115–30.

25. The city was also unable to collect interest from local banks handling public funds, as detailed by Robert W. Williams, Jr., "Martin Behrman and New Orleans Civic Development, 1904–1920," *Louisiana History* 2 (1961): 373–400.

26. The New Orleans Association of Commerce *Yearbook* (New Orleans: publisher unknown, 1913), Print Books and Serials, Louisiana Research Collection, Tulane University. The collaboration between elites in promoting the association's vision is referenced in Anthony Stanonis, *Creating the Big Easy: New Orleans and the Emergence of Modern Tourism, 1918–1945* (Athens: University of Georgia Press, 2006), 30–3.

27. "Picture Patriotism," *The Daily Picayune*, December 15, 1913, 7; "Correspondence," *The Moving Picture World* 17 (1913): 654.

28. "To Reproduce 'Battle of New Orleans,'" *The Moving Picture World* 21 (1914): 1517.

29. "Photoplay Plan," *The Daily Picayune*, January 30, 1914, 6. Paragon is listed as an itinerant film company in the early period, with offices in Mobile, Waterloo, Springfield, Topeka, Kansas City, Galveston, Austin, and Wasau, as well as New Orleans. See Caroline Frick, "Itinerant Filmography, North America," *The Moving Image* 10 (2010): 176.

30. "Picturing the City," *The Daily Picayune*, January 12, 1909, 5 (my emphasis added).

31. "Rex Reaches Royal City," *The Daily Picayune*, February 20, 1912, 3. To this point, Lyman Howe's director C. R. Bosworth further had built a reputation as a "businessman" who assisted Howe's bottom line by contracting industrial films around the country, as told in Arthur Edwin Krows, "Motion Pictures Not for Theater," *Educational Screen* 19 (1940): 235.

32. "Picturing the City," *The Daily Picayune*, January 12, 1909, 5.

33. W.H., "The Moving Picture in the South," *The Moving Picture World* 11 (1912): 107.

34. Advertisement, *The Moving Picture World* 5 (1909): 703, 833; Advertisement, *The Moving Picture World* 4 (1909): 323.

35. "Pictures and Politics," *The Moving Picture World* 14 (1912): 537.

36. "First Photoplay Located Here Has Old Jockey Club for a Background," *The Daily Picayune*, March 16, 1912, 4; Branan, "Movies: The Little Sister"; Advertisement, *The Moving Picture World* 12 (1912): 602. Stuart Holmes, who would go on to perform a famed close-up shot in a D. W. Griffith film, played lead in *A Bucktown Romance*.

37. "Getting Chatty," *Moving Picture World* 13 (1912): 137.

38. See, for example, the analysis of a nineteenth-century travelogue that helped construct these myths of the city in Jennie Lightweiss-Goff, "*Peculiar and Characteristic*: New Orleans's Exceptionalism from Frederick Olmsted to the Deluge," *American Literature* 86 (2014): 147–69.

39. Richard Campanella, *Bienville's Dilemma: A Historical Geography of New Orleans* (Lafayette: University of Louisiana at Lafayette, 2008), 284.

40. Emily Landau, *Spectacular Wickedness: Sex, Race, and Memory in Storyville, New Orleans* (Baton Rouge, LA: LSU Press, 2013), 166–7.

41. Branan, "Movies: The Little Sister," 31.

42. "The Loiterer," *The Daily Picayune*, November 24, 1912, 42.

43. Branan, "Movies: The Little Sister."

44. "Theaters in New Orleans," *The Moving Picture World* 14 (1915): 103.

45. These juxtapositions are laid out forcefully in Matt Sakakeeny, "New Orleans Music as a Circulatory System," *Black Music Research Journal* 31 (2011): 291–325.

46. Erish, *Col. Selig*, 94–8.

47. On the rise and decline of biracial unions in the city, see Eric Arnesen, *Waterfront Workers of New Orleans: Race, Class, and Politics, 1863–1923* (New York: Oxford University Press, 1991).

48. LeSoir was quoted talking about his preferred audience and film subjects in "News and Notables at the New Orleans Hotels," *The Daily Picayune*, February, 28, 1912, 7. His perspective seems counter to numerous correspondences cautioning that pro-northern Civil War films could incite whites to riot in the city and region. See Ernst Boehringer, "Let Sleeping Dogs Lie," *The Moving Picture World* 5 (1909): 129; "Diplomacy in the Plays," *The Moving Picture World* 4 (1909): 152; and W. Wilson, "Some Kindly Criticisms," *The Moving Picture World* 9 (1911): 551; "Observations by Our Man About Town," *The Moving Picture World* 4 (1910): 1041.

49. "Films Voudou and Hoodoo," *The Moving Picture World* 23 (1915): 1959; "Society in Coquille Film," *The Moving Picture World* 23 (1915): 1803. Plaissetty soon reemerged as a film director in New York. See "Plaissetty with Blache," *The Moving Picture World* 24 (1915): 1920; and Richard Abel, *The Ciné Goes to Town, 1896-1914* (Berkeley: University of California Press, 1998), 48.

50. "First Photoplay Located Here Has Old Jockey Club for a Background," *The Daily Picayune*, March 16, 1912, 4.

51. "Coquille Settles Suit," *The Moving Picture World* 23 (1915): 861.

52. Flo Field, "Plans to Make 'NOLA' Films Famous the World Over," *The Times-Picayune*, December 20, 1914, 31.

53. "Film Company Relieved of Suit Attorney Admits Concern Is in Strong Financial Condition," *The Times-Picayune*, January 21, 1915, 4.

54. "Motion Picture Paradise," *The Times-Picayune*, January 27, 1915, 6.

55. "Film Company Relieved of Suit Attorney," 4.

56. Field, "Plans to Make 'NOLA' Films."

57. I tell a more detailed history of Holmes and the local real estate market in Bayou St. John in Vicki Mayer, "The Follies of a Film Economy," *Louisiana Cultural Vistas*, May 2015, 70–3. The public announcement of Holmes's prices were embedded in "Real Estate Men Expect Activity in the Suburbs," *The Daily Picayune*, December 27, 1914, 40.

58. "New Orleans Welcomes NOLA," *Motography* 14 (1915): 1348; see also [Note], *Motography* 14 (1915): 1196.

59. Examples of the special favors afforded film-studio developers abound during the period. See "Roskam Reports Progress," *The Moving Picture World* 22 (1914): 1373; "Notes of the Trade," *The Moving Picture World* 22 (1914): 1399; and "Mayor Behrman Hospitable to Picture Makers," *The Moving Picture World* 24 (1915): 431. Other information gathered from "Gulf Stream Briefs," *The Moving Picture World* 24 (1915): 431; Advertisement, *The Moving Picture World* 30 (1916): 456; and "Amusement," *The Times-Picayune*, May 22, 1915, 4.

60. "Oh, Yes, This Town Is Really Alive," *The Daily Picayune*, May 6, 1913, 2; "City Developing Star Boosters," *The Daily Picayune*, May 9, 1913, 6; "Nola Offering at Columbia Theater," *The Times-Picayune*, April 30, 1916, 8; Abel, *The Ciné Goes to Town*, 48; William M. Hannon, *The Photodrama: Its Place among the Fine Arts* (New Orleans: Ruskin, 1915). A 1902 pamphlet for the Southern Gulf Coast Yachting Association described the younger Hannon as "an extensive holder of realty" who is "extensively engaged in the contracting business," according to the Hancock County Historical Society, "Alphabet File Page 38," accessed May 30, 2011, http://www.hancockcountyhistoricalsociety.com/reference/alphabetfile.htm.

61. William Parrill, "The Nola Film Company and the Diamond Film Company with Some Notes on the Film Writings of William Morgan Hannon," *Regional Dimensions: Studies of Southeast Louisiana* 7 (1989): 67.

62. "Photoplay Air Misty," *The Times-Picayune*, February 20, 1916, 28. The press release was titled "Photoplay Manufacturer Sees Approach of Benefits Denied from Newspaper Advertising of Features," *The Daily Picayune*, February 15, 1916, 11.

63. "Premiere Presentation of Nola Film Company Feature Wins Instant Public Approbation," *The Daily Picayune*, January 23, 1916, 26. See also "Critical Public Puts Stamp of Approval upon New Orleans Manufactured Photodramatic Products," *The Daily Picayune*, May 7, 1916, 42; "Nola Films Show City as a Movie Point," *New Orleans Item*, April 16, 1916, 38; "Photoplay Stars in Local Pictures," *The Times-Picayune*, August 29, 1916, 5; "New Orleans Public Given Opportunity to Pass Judgment on Local Photoplay Productions," *The Daily Picayune*, April 23, 1916, 36.

64. Advertisement, *The Daily Picayune*, April 16, 1916, 30.

65. Allen Scott, *Geography and Economy* (Oxford: Clarendon, 2006), 49–86.

66. Peter Decherney, *Hollywood and the Culture Elite: How the Movies Became American* (New York: Columbia University Press, 2012), 5–6. As an aside illustrating the power of the New York ties to Wall Street, D. W. Griffith created a "whopper myth" in the New York trade press that his unfinanced film *Birth of a Nation* (1915) had earned millions, which it had not, but the nonetheless got Wall Street investors to finance films made in the West. See Janet Wasko, "D. W. Griffith and the Banks: A Case Study in Film Financing," in *The Hollywood Film Industry*, ed. Paul Kerr (London: Routledge & Kegan Paul, 1986), 31–42.

67. "Coquille Changes Release Arrangements," *The Moving Picture World* 24 (1915): 1652; "Nola Offering at Columbia Theater," *The Times-Picayune*; "Nola Film Bookings," *The Times-Picayune*, May 18, 1916, 43; "Camera Eye Sees Defects in Defenses at Panama Canal, and Eye of Camera Furnishes Society Diversions," *The Times-Picayune*, August 20, 1916, 20. Little is known of the Associated Film Sales Corporation of America, the distribution company Hannon signed with. It was said to represent several independent manufacturers in 1915 but became part of a scandal of alleged mail fraud in which the company accepted negatives but refused to distribute films when the manufacturers would not pay for services in the form of stock investments. These charges do not seem to have resulted in anything. In his testimony, Associated's manager oddly implicated Nola Film as one of the companies trying to drive him out of business. See *Hearings before the Committee on the Judiciary, House of Representatives, Sixty-Fourth Congress, First Session, and a Special Subcommittee Thereof, Designated to Investigate Charges against H. Snowden Marshall, U.S. District Attorney for the Southern District of New York* (Washington, DC: Government Printing Office, 1916), 517.

68. Ernest Lee Jahncke, *Annual Report of the New Orleans Association of Commerce*, January 7, 1918.

69. "Orleans May Be 'Movie' Center," *New Orleans Item*, November 25, 1917, 21.

70. "New Orleans Is Announced to Become Permanent Location for Making Program Pictures," *The Times-Picayune*, March 31, 1918, 43.

71. *Diamond Film Company, Incorporated* [investor handbook] (New Orleans, LA: Standard Printing Works, 1917).

72. *New Orleans, Louisiana. Metropolis of the South. Gateway to the Mississippi Valley* (New Orleans: New Orleans Press Club, 1916), 72; "NOLA Film Bookings," *Times-Picayune*; "'NOLA' Films Show City as Movie Point," *New Orleans Item*.

73. "Film Company Charges Another Owes It Money," *New Orleans Item*, March 29, 1919, 3; "Diamond Film Company Faces Receivership," *New Orleans Item*, March 29, 1919, 9;

"Receivership Threatens Diamond Film Company," *The Times-Picayune*, March 29, 1919, 15; Advertisement, *The Times-Picayune*, September 28, 1919, 32.

74. The original embezzlement suit was reported in "Charges of 'High Finance' Alleged in $107,838 Suit," *The Times-Picayune*, December 14, 1917, 7. The final rulings were detailed in "The Decisions of the Supreme and Appellate Courts of Alabama, and the Supreme Courts of Florida, Louisiana, and Mississippi," *The Southern Reporter* 82 (1920): 202–4.

75. "Diamond Theater Company Purchases the People's Theater," *The New Orleans States*, September 9, 1917, 13; Announcement, *The Times-Picayune*, June 8, 1918, 12; "Donaldsonville Canal Bids Before Board," *New Orleans Item*, February 14, 1915, 6; "New Realty Company," *The Times-Picayune*, February 13, 1918, 10. The sales of the new realty company were recorded in the notarial archives of Theodore Beck, Parish of Orleans, 1900–40.

76. Field, "Plans to Make 'NOLA' Films."

77. "Country Club Sold To Robert F. Werk; Handsome Property on Bayou St. John Brings $18,800," *The Times-Picayune*, March 1, 1916, 13. Holmes seemed to have his own checkered past, including gambling and horse-racing interests, which may have affected his asking price and his sudden and unexplained departure. Special thanks to Heidi Schmalbach and Peggy Pond for their research assistance in the New Orleans Notarial Archives.

78. Advertisement, *The New Orleans States*, October 14, 1917, 26; Advertisement, *The New Orleans States*, October 21, 1917, 26; Advertisement, *The New Orleans States*, October 28, 1917, 26; "Diamond Film Company to Make Films in New Orleans Soon," *The New Orleans Item*, April 17, 1918, 14; "New Orleans Is Announced to Become Permanent Location for Making Program Pictures," *The Times-Picayune*, March 31, 1918, 43; Advertisement, *The New Orleans Item*, April 28, 1918, 32. Among Diamond's touted successes were *The Lone Wolf* (1917), directed by Herbert Brenon, and an Alla Nazimova film for the Metro Corporation.

79. It is unclear how many operators were part of the union or how they were represented across the theaters. "New Orleans Trouble," *The Moving Picture World* 22 (1914): 929–30, 1103. Reprinted letters to *The Moving Picture World* from 1912 to 1914 complained of long hours, low wages, and short tenures to prevent promotions. One such projectionist disclosed that the pay was so low that most night projectionists held day jobs as well. He wrote to inquire about a training handbook, suggesting that workers taught themselves technical skills needed for even sub-par employment. "From New Orleans," *The Moving Picture World* 18 (1913): 261.

80. "Work Hard for Benefit," *The Daily Picayune*, July 20, 1913, 42; "Coquille Film Company to Release First Local Production Tuesday," *The Times-Picayune*, May 18, 1915, 4. Among those talents who left was Julian Lemothe, founder of the local chapter of screenplay writers; and Leatrice Joy Zeidler, who went on to Wilkes-Barre, Pennsylvania, before becoming just "Leatrice Joy" in Hollywood. See "Julian Lamothe Visiting Parents," *The Times-Picayune*, December 20, 1917, 23; and [no title], *The Moving Picture World* 23 (1915): 1009. The exodus of local talent to Hollywood and Broadway as well as the city's independent theater history is told in *Le Petit Théâtre du Vieux Carré, New Orleans, La.: An Illustrated Expository and Narrative Account of the Theatre from Its Inception in March, 1916* (New Orleans: Press of Sam W. Taylor, 1928). The newspaper film contest began in March 1916. It ran for months as a way to boost subscriptions, and resulted in the film *Louisiana Lou* (1916). See "Which of These Will Be 'Movie' Stars?," *The Times-Picayune*, March 19, 1916, 35; "Photoplay Banquet for Newspaper Men," *The Daily Picayune*, March 19, 1916, 15.

81. Michael Storper and Susan Christopherson, "Flexible Specialization and Regional Industrial Agglomerations: The Case of the U.S. Motion Picture Industry," *Annals of the Association of American Geographers* 77 (1987): 104–17.

82. Stephanie Frank, "Claiming Hollywood: Boosters, the Film Industry, and Metropolitan Los Angeles," *Journal of Urban History* 38 (2012): 71–88.

83. Andy Pratt, "Creative Cities: The Cultural Industries and the Creative Class," *Geografiska Annaler, Series B: Human Geography* 90 (2008): 107–17.

84. David Goldfield, *Region, Race, and Cities: Interpreting the Urban South* (Baton Rouge, LA: LSU Press, 1997), 67.

85. The most infamous scandal involved the Louisiana LIFT Corporation, which sold millions of state dollars in tax credits for films that would never be realized. See Gordon Russell, "Bagman in Louisiana Film Scandal Sentenced to 10 Months in Prison," *The Times-Picayune*, July 16, 2009, accessed April 7, 2013, http://www.nola.com/.

CHAPTER 2. HOLLYWOOD SOUTH: STRUCTURAL TO VISCERAL REORGANIZATIONS OF SPACE

1. Wilborn Hampton, "An Unlikely Movie Mecca," *The New York Times*, December 29, 1997; Andrew Paxman, "'Sins' Revises Miami's TV Image," *Variety*, April 30, 1998, 17; Keith Dustan, "Movie Magic of Melbourne," *The Age*, February 25, 1992, 9; Bruce McDougall, "Dream Makers Coming to Town," *The Daily Telegraph Mirror*, July 21, 1995; Bradley Graham, "In Argentina, Cinema's Time to Shine," *The Washington Post*, May 4, 1986, H1;

Holly Morris, "Made in Georgia Lower Costs, Gorgeous Scenery Lure Filmmakers to Peach State," *The Atlanta Journal-Constitution*, June 9, 1997, 3B.

2. Terry O'Connor, "Cutting Film Tax Incentives in Louisiana Now Is Short-Sighted State Proposal," *City Business News*, May 16, 2005, 15.

3. Susan Christopherson and Jennifer Clark, *Remaking Regional Economies: Power, Labor and Firm Strategies in the Knowledge Economy* (London: Routledge, 2009), 6.

4. Doreen Massey, *Space, Place and Gender* (Minneapolis: University of Minnesota Press, 1994), 149.

5. J. Mark Souther, *New Orleans on Parade: Tourism and the Transformation of the Crescent City* (Baton Rouge, LA: LSU Press, 2013), 28.

6. See Lynnell Thomas, *Desire and Disaster in New Orleans: Tourism, Race, and Historical Memory* (Durham, NC: Duke University Press, 2014), 17–22, 30–1; Souther, *New Orleans on Parade*, 15–37. The predecessor to the current governing body over tourism was the Greater New Orleans Tourism and Convention Commission.

7. Lance Hill quoted in Gary Rivlin, *Katrina: After the Flood* (New York: Simon and Schuster, 2015), 59. See also excellent accounts of this upward redistribution in countless articles in *The Nation, Slate, Huffington Post, Jacobin*, and *The New York Times*.

8. Dan Baum, "The Lost Year," *The New Yorker*, August 21, 2006, 46.

9. Thomas J. Adams, "How the Ruling Class Remade New Orleans," *Jacobin*, August 29, 2015, accessed February 24, 2016, https://www.jacobinmag.com/2015/08/hurricane-katrina-ten-year-anniversary-charter-schools/.

10. Leo C. Rosten, *Hollywood: The Movie Colony* (New York: Harcourt and Brace, 1941). My reading of Rosten is supplemented here by the perceptive analyses by John Sullivan,

"Leo C. Rosten's Hollywood: Power, Status and the Primacy of Economic and Social Networks in Cultural Production," in *Production Studies: Cultural Studies of Media Industries,* eds. Vicki Mayer, Miranda Banks, and John Caldwell (New York: Routledge, 2009), 39–53; and Vincent Brook, *Land of Smoke and Mirrors: A Cultural History of Los Angeles* (New Brunswick, NJ: Rutgers University Press, 2013).

11. Tom O'Regan, Ben Goldsmith, and Susan Ward, *Local Hollywood: Global Film Production and the Gold Coast* (Brisbane, Australia: University of Queensland Press, 2010), 22.

12. John T. Caldwell, "Para-Industry: Researching Hollywood's Blackwaters," *Cinema Journal* 52 (2013): 157–65.

13. Ibid., 160.

14. Louisiana Motion Picture Incentive Act, Louisiana Acts 1990, Act 480, section 1122, paragraph 1 (approved by Governor, July 18, 1990).

15. Ibid. My emphasis added.

16. These included Arkansas, Rhode Island, and South Carolina.

17. O'Regan et al., *Local Hollywood,* 154.

18. Souther, *New Orleans on Parade,* 159–84.

19. Senate Bill 108, Act 6 2002 La. ALS 6. My emphasis added.

20. Act 551 SB 896 2003 La.

21. Act 456, HB 731 2005. The law allowed tax credits for the building of filmmaking infrastructure "in order to achieve an independent, self-supporting industry." This could apply to production or post-production facilities and could include activities related to set construction and operation, wardrobes, makeup, accessories, photography, sound synchronization or mixing, lighting, editing or film processing, rental of facilities, leasing vehicles, costs of food and lodging, digital or special effects, payroll, music (if performed by a Louisiana musician or released by a Louisiana company), airfare or insurance (if purchased through a local agency). The only things not included were post-production marketing expenses for indirect costs. The language was so broad that it was modified in 2009 to apply to projects only after 50 percent of the project was completed.

22. The relocation provision was part of Act 1240 HB 892 2003, while the time mandate was part of Act 456 HB 731 2005.

23. Act 551 SB 896 2003 La establishes the statewide role, while a variety of local agencies have sprung up to capture the local marketing angle for tourism.

24. Tim Mathis, "Louisiana Tax Credits: Costly Giveaways to Hollywood," *Louisiana Budget Project,* accessed June 10, 2013, http://www.labudget.org/lbp/wp-content/uploads/2012/08/LBP-Report.Louisiana-Film-Tax-Credits.pdf.

25. Helen Morgan Parmett, "Disneyomatics: Media, Branding, and Urban Space in Post-Katrina New Orleans," *Mediascape,* winter 2012, accessed February 24, 2016, http://www.tft.ucla.edu/mediascape/Winter2012_Disneyomatics.html.

26. Christopherson and Clark, *Remaking Regional Economies,* 26. See also Sharon Zukin, *The Culture of Cities* (Malden, MA: Blackwell, 1995).

27. Frank Donze and Gordon Russell, "Four Months to Decide Future Footprint," *The Times-Picayune,* January 11, 2006, 1A. These contractors included the Shaw Group and Blackwater. Their activities and the reactions of local residents to resist them are detailed in Vincanne Adams, *Markets of Sorrow, Labors of Faith: New Orleans in the Wake of Katrina* (Durham, NC: Duke University Press, 2013).

28. Kevin F. Gotham, "Disaster, Inc.: Privatization and Post-Katrina Rebuilding in New Orleans," *Perspectives on Politics* 10 (2012): 641.

29. Richard Sennett, *The Fall of Public Man* (New York: Knopf, 1977).

30. Vicki Mayer and Tanya Goldman, "Hollywood Handouts: Tax Credits in the Age of Economic Crisis," *Jump Cut* 52 (2010), http://www.ejumpcut.org/archive/jc52.2010/mayerTax/text.html.

31. Mayor's Office of Cultural Economy, "Neighborhood Filming Info," *Film New Orleans,* accessed October 6, 2012, http://www.filmneworleans.org/for-filmmakers/production-essentials/neighborhood-filming-info/.

32. Brendan McCarthy, "Biggest Earners in New Orleans Police Details Are Often High-Ranking Officers," *The Times Picayune,* May 15, 2011, accessed September 13, 2012, http://www.lexisnexis.com/hottopics/lnacademic.

33. Jade Miller and I conducted interviews in 2011 and 2012. A more extended treatment of the map study and interviews are presented in a journal-article manuscript currently under review.

34. These films were *Ray* and *The Curious Case of Benjamin Button,* which were shot in the Faubourg Marigny and the Garden District, respectively.

35. All union-member data were received with permission of the president and membership of the local chapter of the International Alliance of Theatrical Stage Employees.

36. I conducted this research with a team that included one postdoctoral and two undergraduate students. Since the city issues paper permits for all public-space uses, including parades and construction, the methodology involved the hand retrieval and entry of all permit information into a computer database in the summer of 2011. From there, we developed a database that standardized location addresses, the duration and extent of use, as well as the variety of city services to be utilized in providing security, safety, or transportation. No personal information was recorded. This database was then drawn into a variegated map using standard geolocational software.

37. David Harvey, *Spaces of Hope* (Berkeley: University of California Press, 2000), 141.

38. This observation is made more generally in a critique of New Orleans's rebuilding after Katrina: "Reinventing the Crescent isn't about the people . . . in Gentilly, St. Bernard Parish, the Upper and Lower Ninth wards," in David Wolff, "'Reinventing the Crescent Reconsidered': Mere Gentrification or Good For Us All?," *The Lens,* August 15, 2013, accessed March 4, 2016, http://thelensnola.org/2013/08/15/reinventing-the-crescent-reconsidered-mere-gentrification-or-good-for-us-all/.

39. "Mansion in the French Quarter, All of Nola at Your Fingertips," *VBRO.com,* accessed December 10, 2014, http://www.vrbo.com/513127. Rental listings for the house could be found on the Internet as recently as March 2015. Other information taken from Mike Scott, "The Whann-Bohn House Near the French Quarter Has a New Life as a Residential Post-Production Facility for Filmmakers," *Nola.com,* September 15, 2012, accessed November 9, 2014, http://www.nola.com/homegarden/index.ssf/2012/09/the_whann-bohn_house_near_the.html; Katherine Sayre, "Esplanade Avenue Film Studio Taken by New Owners after Developers Indicted," *Nola.com,* September 23, 2014, accessed November 11, 2014, http://www.nola.com/business/index.ssf/2014/09/esplanade_avenue_film_studio_t.html#incart_related_stories; Jim Mustian, "Hollywood Producer, His Wife and New Orleans Lawyer Convicted in Scheme to Defraud Louisiana Film Tax Credit Program," *The New Orleans*

Advocate, April 27, 2015, accessed March 4, 2016, http://www.theneworleansadvocate.com/news/12218602–172/3-convicted-in-scheme-to.

40. Cathy Yang Liu, Ric Kolenda, Grady Fitzpatrick, and Tim N. Todd, "Re-creating New Orleans: Driving Development through Creativity," *Economic Development Quarterly* 24 (2010): 221–36.

41. Louise Story, "Michigan Town Woos Hollywood, but Ends Up with a Bit Part," *The New York Times,* December 3, 2012, A1.

42. The introduction of film infrastructure was passed in State House Bill 731, Act 456 (2005). In a personal conversation with Sherry McConnell, she said the policy was never intended to add the proposed 15 percent to the existing 25 percent credit but that is what happened in practice.

43. Loren C. Scott & Associates, Inc., "The Economic Impact of Louisiana's Entertainment Tax Credit Programs," report for the Office of Entertainment Industry Development, Louisiana Department of Economic Development, April 2013, accessed May 1, 2014, http://louisianaentertainment.gov/docs/main/2013_OEID_Program_Impact_Report_(FINAL).pdf.

44. Facts drawn from HR&A Advisors, Inc., "Economic Impacts of the Louisiana Motion Picture Investor Tax Credit," report prepared for the Louisiana Film and Entertainment Industry and the Motion Picture Association of America, April 6, 2015, 66; Kimberly Quillen, "Warehouse Gets Makeover as Film Studio," *AP Newswire,* February 1, 2009, accessed September 13, 2012, http://www.lexisnexis.com/hottopics/lnacademic; "New Markets Tax Credit Investments," CityScape Capital Group LLC, accessed August 25, 2015, http://www.citycapitalscape.com/nmtcprojectdetail.php; Richard A. Webster, "New Orleans Public Housing Remade after Katrina. Is It Working?," *Nola.com,* accessed August 25, 2015, http://www.nola.com/katrina/index.ssf/2015/08/new_orleans_public_housing_dem.html.

45. Elaine Sciolino, "Lumière | Peripheral Vision," *NYT.com,* October 31, 2012, accessed March 4, 2016, http://tmagazine.blogs.nytimes.com/2012/10/31/lumiere-peripheral-vision/.

46. Yang Liu et al., "Re-creating New Orleans," 262, 272.

47. Maps were plotted by neighborhood, city, and state, based on members' self-reported addresses. Identifying names were never provided to me, and address data were disposed after maps were made and shared with the union.

48. David Robb, "Where Hollywood's Union Jobs Are Going: Call These States the Runaway 3," *Deadline,* May 21, 2014, accessed August 25, 2015, http://deadline.com/2014/05/hollywood-runaway-production-tax-credits-georgia-louisiana-iatse-733335/; David Jacobs, "Film Supporters in Baton, New Orleans at Odds over Union Contract," *Baton Rouge Business Report,* April 20, 2015, accessed August 25, 2015, https://www.businessreport.com/article/film-supporters-baton-rouge-new-orleans-odds-union-contract. Wage data from Joel Kotkin, "Sustaining Prosperity: A Long Term Vision for the New Orleans Region," report for Greater New Orleans Inc., February 19, 2014, accessed August 25, 2015, http://gnoinc.org/uploads/Sustaining_Prosperity_Amended_2014_02_16.pdf.

49. Katherine Sayre, "New Orleans Home Prices Up 46 Percent since Hurricane Katrina," *Nola.com,* August 31, 2016, accessed March 4, 2016, http://www.nola.com/business/index.ssf/2015/08/new_orleans_home_prices_up_46.htm; Meghan French-Marcelin, "Gentrification's Ground Zero," *Jacobin,* August 28, 2015, accessed March 4, 2016, https://www.jacobinmag.com/2015/08/katrina-new-orleans-arne-duncan-charters/; Kotkin, "Sustaining

Prosperity"; Gillian White, "The Myth of New Orleans's Affordability," *The Atlantic.com*, July 28, 2015, accessed August 25, 2015, http://www.theatlantic.com/business/archive/2015/07/cities-housing-rental-affordability-new-orleans/399695/; Natalie Chandler, "New Orleans among the Top House Flipping Markets," *New Orleans City Business*, September 30, 2014, accessed August 15, 2015, http://neworleanscitybusiness.com/blog/2014/09/30/new-orleans-among-top-house-flipping-markets/; and Alex Woodward, "New Orleans One of the Worst U.S. Cities for Renters," *Gambit.com*, March 30, 2015, accessed August 15, 2015, http://www.bestofneworleans.com/gambit/new-orleans-one-of-the-worst-us-cities-for-renters/Content?oid = 2609106.

50. Gordon Russell, "Giving Away Louisiana: Film Tax Incentives," *The New Orleans Advocate*, December 12, 2014, accessed August 10, 2015, http://blogs.theadvocate.com/specialreports/2014/12/02/giving-away-louisiana-film-tax-incentives/.

51. Stories on short-term rentals and their prices and locations in the city can be found in Rob Walker, "Airbnb Pits Neighbor against Neighbor in Tourist-Friendly New Orleans," *NYT.com*, March 5, 2016, accessed March 6, 2016, http://www.nytimes.com/2016/03/06/business/airbnb-pits-neighbor-against-neighbor-in-tourist-friendly-new-orleans.html; and Robert McClendon, "What's the Average Air Bnb Making in New Orleans? A Data Miner Finds Out," June 25, 2015, accessed March 4, 2016, http://www.nola.com/politics/index.ssf/2015/06/unauthorized_web_scrape_purpor.html.

52. Eric Hoyt, "Hollywood and the Income Tax, 1929–1955," *Film History* 22 (2010): 5–20.

53. Quin Hillyer, "The Battle for New Orleans," *The American Spectator*, March 9, 2006, accessed March 4, 2016, http://spectator.org/articles/47297/battle-new-orleans. Hollywood celebrities given positive press coverage for their homes in New Orleans include John Goodman, Sandra Bullock, Nicholas Cage, Brad Pitt, Angelina Jolie, and Beyoncé.

54. Shalia Dewan, "New Orleans Restaurant Scene Rises, Reflecting a Richer City," *NYT.com*, December 2, 2013, accessed March 4, 2016, http://www.nytimes.com/2013/12/03/business/rebuilding-new-orleans-one-meal-at-a-time.html?_r = 0.

55. Popular critiques of Richard Florida's consulting enterprise abound. For example, see Joel Kotkin, "Richard Florida Concedes the Limits of the Creative Class," *New Geography*, March 20, 2013, accessed August 25, 2015, http://www.newgeography.com/content/003575-richard-florida-concedes-limits-creative-class. On New Orleans specifically, see French-Marcelin, "Gentrification's Ground Zero"; and Wolff, "Reinventing the Crescent."

56. For example: Joseph Roach, *Cities of the Dead: Circum-Atlantic Performance* (New York: Columbia University Press, 1996); Mick Burns, *Keeping the Beat on the Street: The New Orleans Brass Band Renaissance* (Baton Rouge: LSU Press, 2006); Roger D. Abrahams, Nick Spitzer, John F. Szwed, and Robert Farris Thompson, *Blues for New Orleans: Mardi Gras and America's Creole Soul* (Philadelphia: University of Pennsylvania, 2006); Helen Regis, "Second Lines, Minstrelsy, and the Contested Landscapes of New Orleans Afro-Creole Festivals," *Cultural Anthropologist* 14 (1999): 472–504.

57. Eric Gordon and Adriana de Souza e Silva, *Net Locality: Why Location Matters in a Networked World* (West Sussex, UK: Wiley Blackwell, 2011), 90.

58. Bruce Raeburn, "'They're Tryin' to Wash Us Away': New Orleans Musicians Surviving Katrina," *Journal of American History* 94 (2007): 812–9.

59. Ben Adler, "New Orleans' Transit System Still Hasn't Recovered, 10 Years after Katrina," *Grist.com*, August 19, 2015, accessed March 4, 2016, http://grist.org/cities/new-

orleans-transit-system-still-hasnt-recovered-10-years-after-katrina/; Paul Rioux, "Crescent City Connection, Algiers Ferry Are Hollywood South Favorites," *Nola.com,* August 29, 2011, accessed September 13, 2012, http://www.nola.com/movies/index.ssf/2011/08/crescent_city_connection_algie.html; Owen Courrèges, "Freret Bus Line Sacrificed to Prop Up Loyola Streetcar Numbers," *Uptown Messenger,* April 14, 2014, accessed March 4, 2016, http://uptownmessenger.com/2014/04/owen-courreges-freret-bus-line-sacrificed-to-prop-up-new-loyola-avenue-streetcar-numbers/.

60. Marc Augé, *Non-Places: Introduction to an Anthropology of Supermodernity* (London: Verso, 1995).

61. André Jannson, "Texture: A Key Concept for Communication Geography," *European Journal of Communication* 10 (2006): 185–202.

62. Walter Benjamin, "One Way Street [1928]," in *Walter Benjamin: Selected Writings, Volume I, 1913–1926,* eds. Marcus Bullock and Michael W. Jennings (Cambridge, MA: Belknap of Harvard University Press, 1996), 444–88.

63. Sharon Zukin, *Landscapes of Power: From Detroit to Disney World* (Berkeley: University of California Press, 1991), 28.

64. Ibid., 28–9.

65. A useful critique of Augé's romanticization of non-places as those that conceal hidden labor can be found in Sarah Sharma, "Baring Life and Lifestyle in the Non-Place," *Cultural Studies* 23 (2009): 129–48.

66. Robert McClendon, "New Orleans Tourism Industry Booms but Income Inequality Remains Entrenched," *Nola.com,* October 28, 2014, accessed February 29, 2016, http://www.nola.com/politics/index.ssf/2014/10/new_orleans_tourism_industry_b.html.

67. Christopherson and Clark, *Remaking Regional Economies,* 87.

68. Xiaofei Hao and Chris Ryan, "Interpretation, Film Language and Tourism Destinations," *Annals of Tourism Research* 42 (2013): 334–58; Nick Couldry, *The Place of Media Power* (London: Routledge, 2000).

69. "GO NOLA—The Official Tourism App of the City of New Orleans," I-Tunes, accessed March 4, 2016, https://itunes.apple.com/us/app/go-nola-official-tourism-app/id587077099?mt = 8.

70. Susan Ward and Tom O'Regan, "The Film Producer as the Long-Stay Business Tourist: Rethinking Film and Tourism from a Gold Coast Perspective," *Tourism Geographies* 11 (2009): 214–32.

71. Mike Scott, "Cirque du Freak Wraps Production in Louisiana," *Associated Press Newswire,* June 22, 2008, accessed March 4, 2016, http://www.lexisnexis.com/hottopics/lnacademic. The mirror of the quote is found in "Creative & Digital Media: Your Creative Catalyst," Greater New Orleans Inc., accessed March 4, 2016, http://m.gnoinc.org/media.php.

72. Gwen Filosa, "Some Residents Want *Treme* Series out of the Area," *Associated Press Newswire,* March 27, 2010, accessed September 13, 2012, http://www.lexisnexis.com/hottopics/lnacademic.

73. Information gathered on a film tour in 2013. See also Cara Kelly, "The Big Easy on the Big Screen? Small Wonder," *The Washington Post,* March 11, 2012, F3.

74. Yang Liu et al., *Re-creating New Orleans,* 262.

75. Michel Foucault, "Of Other Spaces: Utopias and Heterotopias (1967)," trans. Jay Miskowiec, *Architecture/Mouvement/Continuité* 5 (1986): 27.

76. See critiques of heterotopias in Harvey, *Spaces of Hope,* and of the new regionalism as a kind of utopic fantasy in Christopherson and Clark, *Remaking Regional Economies.*

CHAPTER 3. THE PLACE OF *TREME* IN THE FILM ECONOMY: LOVE AND LABOR FOR HOLLYWOOD SOUTH

1. Margaret Talbot, "Stealing Life," *The New Yorker,* October 22, 2007, accessed March 4, 2016, http://www.newyorker.com/magazine/2007/10/22/stealing-life.

2. According to the aggregate totals for length and extent of uses derived from the study presented in chapter 2, *Treme* used 11 percent of the public spaces reserved for location shooting, followed by *Cirque du Freak* (2009), *Green Lantern* (2011), and *Black Water Transit* (2009). Expenditures on the pilot can be found in Bax Starr Consulting Group, "Fiscal and Economic Impact Analysis of Louisiana's Entertainment Incentives," report for the Legislative Fiscal Office and the Office of Entertainment Industry Development, Louisiana Department of Economic Development, April 25, 2011, 13.

3. Vincanne Adams, *Markets of Sorrow, Labors of Faith: New Orleans in the Wake of Katrina* (Durham, NC: Duke University Press, 2013), 179.

4. Ibid., 100.

5. David Simon, "David Simon on what HBO's '*Treme*' meant to him and what he hopes it meant to New Orleanians," *Nola.com,* December 27, 2013, accessed December 28, 2013, http://www.nola.com/treme-hbo/index.ssf/2013/12/david_simon_on_what_hbos_treme.html.

6. Nancy Fraser, *Scales of Justice: Reimagining Political Space in a Globalizing World* (New York: Columbia University Press, 2009), 17.

7. Christena E. Nippert-Eng, *Home and Work: Negotiating Boundaries through Everyday Life* (Chicago: University of Chicago Press, 2008).

8. I identify interviewees by the demographic descriptors they shared with me, while preserving anonymity to the extent required by the Tulane University human subjects board.

9. Violet H. Bryan, "Land of Dreams: Image and Reality in New Orleans," *Urban Resources* 1 (1984): 29. See similar discussions of film and television representations of the city in Scott Jordan Harris, *World Film Locations: New Orleans* (Chicago: Intellect, 2012); and Wayne H. Schuth, "The Image of New Orleans on Film," in *The South and Film,* ed. Warren French (Oxford: University of Mississippi Press, 1981), 240–5.

10. Several interviewees in this study talked about Mardi Gras Indians, a vernacular black tradition in the city dating to the early twentieth century. A good history and cultural analysis of this culture is found in George Lipsitz, *Time Passages: Collective Memory and American Popular Culture* (Minneapolis: University of Minnesota Press, 1990).

11. Cynthia Dobbs, "Vernacular Kinship, the Creole City, and Faulkner's 'New Orleans,'" *Faulkner Journal* 26 (2012): 58.

12. These assertions about archives and diasporas draw most heavily on archive theorists who relate them to diasporic and queer histories. See Jacques Derrida, *Archive Fever* (Chicago: University of Chicago Press, 1996); Heather Love, *Feeling Backwards: Loss and the Politics of Queer History* (Cambridge, MA: Harvard University Press, 2007); and Ann Cvetkovich, *An Archive of Feelings: Trauma, Sexuality, and Lesbian Public Cultures* (Durham, NC: Duke University Press, 2003).

13. Sigmund Freud, "Notes on a Mystic Writing Pad [1925]," in *General Psychological Theory* (New York: Touchstone, 1997), 207–12.

14. Lauren Berlant, *Cruel Optimism* (Durham, NC: Duke University Press, 2011), 199–200.

15. Alan Richman, "Yes, We're Open," *GQ Magazine*, November 2, 2006, accessed March 14, 2014, http://www.gq.com/food-travel/alan-richman/200611/katrina-new-orleans-food#ixzz1lHYbr4MI.

16. See Adams, *Markets of Sorrow*, for documentation of this dialectic.

17. Helen Morgan Parmett, *"Down in the Treme": Media's Spatial Practices and the (Re) birth of a Neighborhood after Katrina* (doctoral thesis, University of Minnesota, 2012).

18. David Simon, "Why I Don't Tweet, Example #47," *The Audacity of Despair: Collected Prose, Links, and Occasional Venting from David Simon* (blog), May 15, 2013, accessed May 12, 2014, http://davidsimon.com/why-i-dont-tweet-example-47/.

19. In light of smaller budgets and public calls for corporate social responsibility, the series has shared common cause with other television programming that promises to improve the well-being not just of the audience member, but of the ordinary people brought into the production itself. For example, reality and talk shows were two genres that have frequently promoted how the people on their staffs and crews were part of a family that left local populations better off than before. In the meantime, these programs cut production costs through their appropriation of local settings and enrollment of local residents, often in the form of volunteers. See Laurie Ouellette and James Hay, *Better Living through Reality TV: Television and Post-Welfare Citizenship* (New York: Wiley, 2008).

20. See Mark Banks on moral economies, using Manchester as the place for his case study, "Moral Economy and Cultural Work," *Sociology* 40 (2006): 455–72.

21. Analyses of the historical relationship between studio publicity and extra labor supply can be found in Denise McKenna, "The Photoplay or the Pickaxe: Extras, Gender, and Labour in Early Hollywood," *Film History* 23 (2011): 5–19; Shelley Stamp, "'It's a Long Way to Filmland': Starlets, Screen Hopefuls, and Extras in Early Hollywood," in *American Cinema's Transitional Era: Audiences, Institutions, Practices,* eds. Charlie Keil and Shelley Stamp (Berkeley: University of California Press, 2004), 332–51; and Danae Clark, *Negotiating Hollywood: The Cultural Politics of Actors' Labor* (Minneapolis: University of Minnesota Press, 1995).

22. Lauren Laborde, "Treme Needs You for Fake Jazz Fest," *Gambit.com*, April 29, 2011, accessed March 21, 2016, http://www.bestofneworleans.com/blogofneworleans/archives/2011/04/29/treme-needs-you-for-fake-jazz-fest.

23. John Roberts, *Philosophizing the Everyday: Revolutionary Praxis and the Fate of Cultural Theory* (London: Pluto Press, 2006).

24. Kelly Parker, "New Orleans Is Ready for the New Season of 'Treme,'" *The Louisiana Weekly,* April 19, 2011, accessed March 20, 2016, http://www.louisianaweekly.com/233/, 11.

25. "What I Learned as an Extra on Treme," *Hamm Hawk,* February 22, 2010, accessed March 21, 2016, https://hammhawk.wordpress.com/2010/02/22/what-i-learned-as-an-extra-on-treme/.

26. Laura Grindstaff, "Just Be Yourself—Only More So: Ordinary Celebrity in the Age of Self-Service Television," in *The Politics of Reality TV: Global Perspectives,* eds. Marwan Kraidy and Katherine Sender (New York: Routledge, 2011), 44–57.

27. Elspeth Probyn talks about this sense of being and longing in relation to her identity and Montreal in *Outside Belongings* (London: Routledge, 1996).

28. Probyn, *Outside Belongings*, 13.

29. Elspeth Probyn, "Television's Unheimlich Home," in *The Politics of Everyday Fear*, ed. Brian Massumi (Minneapolis: University of Minnesota Press, 1993), 261–93.

30. Erin Moore Daly, "New Orleans, Invisible City," *Nature and Culture* 1 (2006): 137.

31. Andrew Edgar, "The Uncanny, Alienation and Strangeness: The Entwining of Political and Medical Metaphor," *Medicine, Health Care and Philosophy* 14 (2011): 313–22.

32. This concept is articulated most clearly in Joseph Wagner, "Creole Urbanism: Searching for an Urban Future in the Flooded Streets of New Orleans," *Space and Culture* 9 (2006): 103–6.

33. Pointing his critique at a long line of intellectuals in Latin America, Colás slams intellectuals as intermediaries for a fetishized culture that, absent nonwhite labor and foreign capital, magically produces the "independent Latin American creole subject," who is nonetheless completely dependent on a neocolonial order. See Santiago Colás, "Of Creole Symptoms, Cuban Fantasies, and Other Latin American Postcolonial Ideologies," *PMLA* 110 (1995): 388.

34. The event took place in October 2007 at an evening funeral parade for a murdered musician. It was the basis for the *Treme* episode "Knock With Me, Rock With Me" (season 3).

35. Edgar, "The Uncanny, Alienation, and Strangeness," 321: "Illness experienced as the uncanny may be authentic, but is ultimately a state of resignation. In contrast, illness redeemed as alienation opens the hopeful possibility that social and medical conditions can be changed."

36. Mardi Gras was a central event in three episodes and a recurring motif for various characters over the series' three-and-a-half seasons.

37. Located primarily in the Bywater and Tremé neighborhoods, the music venues featured on *Treme*, such as Vaughn's, Bullets, and the Candlelight Lounge, became regular outposts for cultural heritage tourists over the course of the series. One interviewee called the new customers in those places "Lonely Planeters," referencing a travel guide that markets authentic experiences.

38. Dave Walker, "On the HBO 'Treme' Trail: David Simon and Eric Overmyer Discuss Creation of Prospective Drama," *Nola.com*, April 4, 2009, accessed May 10, 2015, http://blog.nola.com/davewalker/2009/04/on_the_treme_trail_david_simon.html.

39. According to locations manager Virginia McCollam, the production required twenty to thirty locations per shoot, necessitating a wider network with neighborhoods that had not previously had film shooting. See Bridgette Marie Clifton, "Locations, Locations, Locations," *Markee 2.0*, December 7, 2012, accessed March 24, 2016, http://markeemagazine.com/wp/locations-locations-locations-2/.

40. This quote is taken from the promotional website for the documentary *Trouble the Water* (2008), accessed March 24, 2016, http://www.troublethewaterfilm.com/content/pages/the_story/.

41. Michael Curtin and Kevin Sanson, "Precarious Creativity: Global Media, Local Labor," in *Precarious Creativity: Global Media, Local Labor*, eds. Michael Curtin and Kevin Sanson (Berkeley: University of California Press, 2016), 2.

42. Toby Miller, "Cybertarian Flexibility—When the Prosumers Join the Cognitariat, All That Is Scholarship Melts into Air," in *Precarious Creativity: Global Media, Local Labor,* eds. Michael Curtin and Kevin Sanson (Berkeley: University of California Press, 2016), 26.

(ALMOST A) CONCLUSION

1. Elizabeth Crisp, "Bobby Jindal Adviser Suggests Reining in 'Very Expensive' Film Tax Credit Program," *The New Orleans Advocate,* April 6, 2015, accessed May 29, 2015, http://theadvocate.com/news/11891186–123/officials-question-film-tax-credit.

2. One good summary is in Elaine S. Povich, "Some States Yell 'Cut!' on Film Tax Credits," *Huffington Post,* May 18, 2015, accessed April 15, 2016, http://www.huffingtonpost.com/2015/05/18/states-film-tax-credits_n_7306342.html.

3. Heard on WWBZ, 90.7 FM, April 28, 2015, 3 P.M.

4. Tim Mathis, "Louisiana Film Tax Credits: Costly Giveaways to Hollywood," *Louisiana Budget Project,* August 7, 2012, accessed April 16, 2016, http://www.labudget.org/lbp/wp-content/uploads/2012/08/LBP-Report.Louisiana-Film-Tax-Credits.pdf.

5. Posted on Facebook site "Here's my $2," September 30, 2014, accessed May 26, 2015, https://www.facebook.com/heresmytwobucks.

6. "LFEA to Produce a Film!" *WGNO.com,* May 12, 2015, accessed May 26, 2015, http://wgno.com/2015/05/12/lfea-to-produce-a-film/.

7. Louisiana Senate Press Office, "Senator Morrell Seeks to Reform and Streamline State's Film Tax Credits," April 1, 2015, accessed April 16, 2016, http://senate.la.gov/Morrell/releases/2015/040115.pdf.

8. Tyler Bridges, "Louisiana House Panel Favors Capping—but Not Eliminating—Film Tax Credits," *The Advocate,* April 28, 2015, accessed April 3, 2016, http://theadvocate.com/news/12227839–123/house-committee-favors-capping-film.

9. Although the AFP claims they lobby against film tax subsidies in the interest of eliminating all public subsidies for special interests, the Kochs also have funded social campaigns to drive Hollywood out of regions with religious-freedom laws sanctioning homophobia and discrimination. For the various connections between the Koch brothers and Hollywood, see "North Carolina Film Tax Incentives: The Kochs Strike Back," *The Real Koch Facts,* July 18, 2014, accessed April 15, 2016, http://realkochfacts.com/north-carolina-film-tax-incentives-the-afp-strikes-back/; Katy Canada, "Americans for Prosperity Ad Attacks NC Senate's Proposed Film Grants," *The News & Observer,* June 9, 2014, accessed April 15, 2016, http://www.newsobserver.com/news/politics-government/state-politics/article10332998.html; "AFP-FL Saves Floridians Billions in Tax Cuts & Corporate Welfare," *Americans for Prosperity,* March 15, 2016, accessed April 15, 2016, https://americansforprosperity.org/afp-fl-saves-floridians-billions-tax-cuts-corporate-welfare/; Maggie Lee, "Koch-Funded Group Might Target Georgia Film and TV Tax Credit," *Creative Loafing,* April 8, 2016, accessed April 15, 2016, http://clatl.com/freshloaf/archives/2016/04/08/koch-funded-group-might-target-georgia-film-and-tv-tax-credit.

10. Erich Schwartzel and Cameron McWhirter, "Group Backed by Koch Brothers Takes Aim at Tax Credits for Films," *WSJ.com,* March 25, 2016, accessed April 15, 2016, http://www.wsj.com/articles/group-backed-by-koch-brothers-takes-aim-at-tax-credits-for-films-1458934367#livefyre-comment.

11. La. H.B.829 (2015 Regular Session). See also Kevin Litten, "$180M Cap on Film Tax Credits May Kill Hollywood South, Morrell Says," *Nola.com*, June 12, 2015, accessed September 1, 2015, http://www.nola.com/politics/index.ssf/2015/06/senate_kills_film_credit_progr.html; Mark Ballard, "Gov. Bobby Jindal Complimentary of State Budget as He Signs It into Law," *The New Orleans Advocate*, August 20, 2015, accessed September 1, 2015, http://theadvocate.com/news/12695669–124/gov-bobby-jindal-signs-state; Gordon Russell, "New Legislation Puts Limit of $180M on Movie Credit Program," *The New Orleans Advocate*, July 3, 2015, accessed September 1, 2015, http://theadvocate.com/news/neworleans/neworleansnews/12770210–123/new-cap-on-state-tax.

12. Mark Ballard, "New Lawsuits Likely from New Limits on Tax Credit," *The New Orleans Advocate*, June 23, 2015, accessed September 1, 2015, http://theadvocate.com/news/12708043–123/lawsuits-likely-from-new-limits; Kevin Litten, "Film Industry Walks Back Lawsuit Threats, Dire Predictions over Film Tax Credits," *Nola.com*, July 9, 2015, accessed September 1, 2015, http://www.nola.com/politics/index.ssf/2015/07/film_industry_lawsuit_tax_cred.html; Greg Albrecht, "Fiscal Note on HB 829," *Louisiana Legislative Fiscal Office Notes*, July 15, 2015, accessed September 1, 2015, http://www.legis.la.gov/legis/ViewDocument.aspx?d = 959479.

13. Tyler Bridges, "Major Downturn Plagues Louisiana's Film, TV Industry 'Hollywood South' after Big Changes to Tax Credit Program," *The Advocate*, March 26, 2016, accessed April 16, 2016, http://theadvocate.com/news/15300902–63/major-downturn-plagues-louisianas-film-tv-industry-hollywood-south-after-big-changes-to-film-tax-cre.

14. Lane Holman, "Welcome to Y'allywood. We've Got Jobs!," *AJC.com*, January 17, 2015, accessed April 3, 2016, http://www.ajc.com/news/news/local-education/welcome-to-yallywood-weve-got-jobs/njjW9/; Chelsea Bradsted, "California to Triple Film Tax Credits: What Does It Mean for Louisiana?," *Nola.com*, September 5, 2014, accessed April 3, 2016, http://www.nola.com/entertainment/baton-rouge/index.ssf/2014/09/california_to_triple_film_tax.html.

15. Interestingly, Atlanta, the hub of the Georgia film economy, was the only city that ranked worse in income inequality. Robert McClendon, "New Orleans Is Second Worst for Income Inequality in the U.S., Roughly on Par with Zambia, Report Says," *Nola.com*, August 19, 2014, accessed April 15, 2016, http://www.nola.com/politics/index.ssf/2014/08/new_orleans_is_2nd_worst_for_i.html; White, "The Myth of New Orleans's Affordability."

16. Web pages that Labry curates include http://www.louisianasunshine.net/, https://www.facebook.com/louisianasunshine, and https://www.facebook.com/keeplouisianafilmindustry/, last accessed April 15, 2016.

17. Peter Nowalk and Hillary Stamm, *The Hollywood Assistants Handbook: 86 Rules for Aspiring Power Players* (New York: Workman, 2008).

18. Barbara Ehrenreich, *Bright-Sided: How the Relentless Pursuit of Positive Thinking Has Undermined America* (New York: Metropolitan Books, 2009), 8–9.

19. Although this has been stated in various ways throughout the literatures on autonomous labor and creative economy, it has only recently become news via a *New York Times Magazine* piece written by a National Public Radio reporter. See Adam Davidson, "What Hollywood Can Teach Us about the Future of Work," *The New York Times Magazine*, May 5, 2015, accessed May 29, 2015, http://www.nytimes.com/2015/05/10/magazine/what-hollywood-can-teach-us-about-the-future-of-work.html.

20. Isabell Lorey, *State of Insecurity: Government of the Precarious* (London: Verso, 2015), 1.

21. Ibid., 84.

22. Film L.A. Inc., "2013 Feature Film Production Report," Film L.A. Research, 6, accessed July 1, 2014, http://www.filmla.com/data_reports.php.

23. The research firm contracted by LFEA and the MPAA reports a number that nearly doubles the six thousand or so jobs actually certified by the state government yearly. See HR&A Advisors, Inc., "Economic Impacts of the Louisiana Motion Picture Investor Tax Credit," report prepared for the Louisiana Film and Entertainment Industry and the Motion Picture Association of America, April 6, 2015.

24. Tyler Bridges, "Film Industry Tax-Credits Study Reports Many Benefits for Louisiana; Critics Not Convinced Credits Are Worth the Cost," *The New Orleans Advocate,* April 10, 2015, accessed May 26, 2015, http://theadvocate.com/news/12036883–123/film-industry-claims-tax-credit; Louisiana Film and Entertainment Association, "Statewide Survey Showcases Public Opinion of Louisiana's Film Industry" April 20, 2015, accessed May 26, 2015, https://lfea.org/wp-content/uploads/2015/04/Press-Release-LSU-Ombibus-Survey.pdf.

25. France "Bifo" Berardi, *The Uprising: On Poetry and Finance* (Los Angeles, CA: Semiotext(e), 2012), 140.

26. Ibid., 167.

27. Examples of these social movements in New Orleans include the Restaurant Opportunities Center, the local Fight for Fifteen, Blights Out, and the New Orleans Musicians Clinic.

28. Shannon Muchmore, "Breaking the System: State Budget Battles Gut Healthcare for the Most Vulnerable," *Modern Healthcare,* April 23, 2016, accessed April 25, 2016, http://www.modernhealthcare.com/article/20160423/MAGAZINE/304239988;   Marissa DeCuir, "Board Declares Exigency for UNO," *LSUNow,* April 24, 2016, accessed April 25, 2016,   http://www.lsunow.com/board-declares-exigency-for-uno/article_7838b7cb-db5c-5418–82c8-a67d8b8eaaa7.html.

29. Good examples of media making in support of horizontal forms of social-movement organizing can be found in Sasha Costanza-Chock, *Out of the Shadows, Into the Streets! Transmedia Organizing and the Immigrant Rights Movement* (Cambridge, MA: MIT Press, 2014).

30. Sources of news and advocacy for these laws are Creative Minnesota, Missouri Citizens for the Arts, and the Arts Creative Advocacy Network in Portland. I especially thank Jeanne Nathan of the Creative Alliance for New Orleans (CANO) for providing a knowledge clearinghouse for policy directions that different locales have taken in support of arts and cultural production.

APPENDIX

1. Scott's neoliberal politics is expressed in numerous presentations and interviews posted to the Internet, as well as in scholarly articles dating back at least to the early 1980s. See, for example, Loren C. Scott and James Richardson, "Government Regulation and Market Distortion: The Case of the NGPA and the Louisiana Economy," *Journal of Energy and Development* 8 (1982): 59–72.

2. See Loren C. Scott & Associates, Inc., "The Economic Impact of Louisiana's Entertainment Tax Credit Programs," report for the Office of Entertainment Industry Development, Louisiana Department of Economic Development, April 2013, accessed May 1, 2014, http://louisianaentertainment.gov/docs/main/2013_OEID_Program_Impact_Report_(FINAL).pdf; and HR&A Advisors, Inc., "Comparison of Loren Scott Analysis and HR&A Analysis," report for the Louisiana Film and Entertainment Association and Motion Picture Association of America, April 2015, accessed May 15, 2015, http://www.mpaa.org/wp-content/uploads/2015/04/Louisiana-HRA-Review-of-Loren-Scott-Study.pdf.

3. Scott and Associates, Inc., "The Economic Impact," v.

4. Ibid., 14.

5. Mike McLaughlin, "More on Multipliers in Evaluating the Economic Impacts of Movies," *North Carolina Insight* (February 1993): 11.

6. Scott and Associates, Inc., "The Economic Impact," 18.

7. Ibid., 14.

8. Ibid., 17.

INDEX

CPSIA information can be obtained
at www.ICGtesting.com
Printed in the USA
BVOW07s2346150917
495019BV00006B/59/P